# AUGUSTUS SAINT-GAUDENS

## IN THE METROPOLITAN MUSEUM OF ART

### THAYER TOLLES

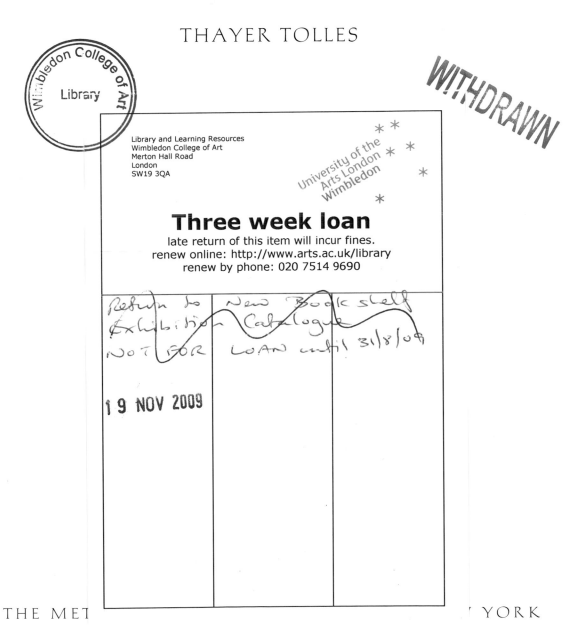
THE MET YORK

YALE UNIVERSITY PRESS, NEW HAVEN AND LONDON

Reprint of *The Metropolitan Museum of Art Bulletin* (Spring 2009).
Copyright © 2009 by The Metropolitan Museum of Art, New York

This publication is made possible through the generosity of the Lila Acheson Wallace Fund
for The Metropolitan Museum of Art, established by the cofounder of *Reader's Digest*.

Additional support has been provided by the William Cullen Bryant Fellows.

This publication is issued in conjunction with the exhibition "Augustus Saint-Gaudens in
The Metropolitan Museum of Art," held at The Metropolitan Museum of Art, New York,
from June 30 to November 15, 2009.

The Eugénie Prendergast Exhibitions of American Art are made possible by a grant from
Jan and Warren Adelson.

Publisher and Editor in Chief: John P. O'Neill
Editor of the *Bulletin:* Sue Potter
Production: Christopher Zichello
Design: Bruce Campbell

Cover: Augustus Saint-Gaudens (American, 1848–1907). *Victory*, 1892–1903 (this cast, 1914 or after, by 1916);
see fig. 47, page 41. This page: Augustus Saint-Gaudens. *Rodman de Kay Gilder*, 1879 (this cast, probably 1880),
detail of cipher; see cat. 12, page 64.

New photography of works in The Metropolitan Museum of Art is by Bruce Schwarz, The Photograph Studio.
Fig. 61 is from the MMA Archives. We are grateful to the United States Department of the Interior, National
Park Service, Saint-Gaudens National Historic Site, Cornish, New Hampshire, for supplying figs. 1, 2, 8, 10,
21–23, 25, 28, 29, 32, 38–40, 44, 49, 52, and 57–59. Fig. 24 is courtesy of Chicago Park District. Fig. 51 is from
Lorado Taft, "American Sculpture at the Exposition, II," *Brush and Pencil* 6 (August 1900), p. 215. Other
photographs were supplied by the institutions and individuals named in the captions. Credit is due to the
following photographers: Glenn Castellano: fig. 33; Kevin Daley: fig. 53; Francis Dzikowski: fig. 14 (photograph
© 2008 by Francis Dzikowski/Esto); Jeffrey Nintzel: fig. 44; James Peterson: fig. 24; David Stansbury: fig. 26;
Gordon Sweet: fig. 17 (courtesy of the Saint-Gaudens National Historic Site); Jerry L. Thompson: fig. 20; and
Graydon Wood: fig. 41.

For a complete record of inscriptions on objects included in the Exhibition Checklist (pages 61–79), see the
American Paintings and Sculpture collection database at www.metmuseum.org.

Cataloging-in-Publication data is available from the Library of Congress.
ISBN 978-1-58839-320-3 (The Metropolitan Museum of Art)
ISBN 978-0-300-15188-6 (Yale University Press)

Printed and bound in Singapore.

# Director's Note

To late nineteenth-century Americans Augustus Saint-Gaudens was well known as a sculptor of public monuments rendered in a naturalistic, vital, and thoroughly modern aesthetic. A son of French-Irish immigrants, Saint-Gaudens (1848–1907) embodied the American success story, rising from humble Lower East Side circumstances to become the finest American sculptor of his day, attracting international acclaim and patronage. Born in Dublin, Ireland, he was the quintessential cosmopolite artist—during his four-decade career he moved effortlessly between studios in New York, Paris, Rome, and his beloved Cornish, New Hampshire. He counted among his friends a cultural who's who: writers Henry James and William Dean Howells, artists John Singer Sargent and Maxfield Parrish, and architects Stanford White and Charles McKim, and his clients included Cornelius Vanderbilt II and President Theodore Roosevelt. But Saint-Gaudens always remained self-effacing, quipping that it was his exotic name (as he said, pronounced Gaudens, as in "gaudy") as much as his sculptures that brought him distinction. Whether or not his name is as broadly familiar today, his art remains celebrated and relevant, from the gilded equestrian monument of William Tecumseh Sherman in New York to the storied twenty-dollar "double eagle" gold piece he designed for President Roosevelt.

The Metropolitan's collection of works by Saint-Gaudens numbers 45—in marble, bronze, plaster, terracotta, and even shell. His association with the Museum is reflected not only in these tangible objects but also through his career-long connections with its staff and trustees and their tireless efforts to assemble a comprehensive memorial exhibition of 154 works in the Great Hall in 1908. In subsequent years, a representative group of Saint-Gaudens's sculptures entered the collection through astute purchases and generous gifts and bequests. Now, just over one hundred years after the artist's death, the Metropolitan's holdings of his works continue to grow steadily, affirming the adage "adding strength to strength." Saint-Gaudens's engaging story and his substantial legacy at the Metropolitan are detailed in this issue of the *Bulletin*, written by Thayer Tolles, Associate Curator in the Department of American Paintings and Sculpture.

This *Bulletin* accompanies an exhibition of the same title that will be on view in the Museum's Erving and Joyce Wolf Gallery in the New American Wing from June 30 through November 15, 2009. Fittingly, the exhibition of 80 works will be the first held in the American Wing following the reopening of the Charles Engelhard Court in May 2009. Five sculptures by Saint-Gaudens have been installed in the court among the Museum's unparalleled collection of American monumental sculpture, making it a particularly auspicious moment to commemorate Saint-Gaudens and American sculpture at the Metropolitan. We salute the institutions and collectors who have kindly shared their Saint-Gaudens sculptures with our visitors, enabling us to offer an even fuller account of the career of this remarkable artist and his indelible role in this institution's long-standing commitment to promoting American sculpture. The exhibition is the latest in the distinguished series The Eugénie Prendergast Exhibitions of American Art, made possible by a grant from longtime American Wing supporters Jan and Warren Adelson.

Thomas P. Campbell
*Director*

# AUGUSTUS SAINT-GAUDENS IN THE METROPOLITAN MUSEUM OF ART

*Epic poet of bronze*—so the *New York Herald* hailed Augustus Saint-Gaudens the day after his memorial exhibition opened at The Metropolitan Museum of Art on March 2, 1908. The most accomplished American sculptor of his time, Saint-Gaudens (fig. 1) redirected the course of the medium in the United States: from an Italian Neoclassical to a French-inspired aesthetic, from traditional to American subjects, and from marble as the preferred material to bronze, which so perfectly suited his expressive sculptural technique that the metal itself became central to the ethos of his work. Through some two hundred projects, twenty of them major monuments, Saint-Gaudens energized and modernized the art of sculpture and broadened its audience, making it a part of Americans' day-to-day experience. The entire arc of his life and career can be traced through his public sculptures and through the Metropolitan's substantial holdings of his work.

Saint-Gaudens was born on March 1, 1848, in Dublin, Ireland, to a French-born father, Bernard Paul Ernest Saint-Gaudens (1816–1893), and an Irish mother, Mary McGuiness (d. 1875) from County Longford. Six months later the family arrived in the United States, joining the wave of immigrants escaping famine in Ireland. They settled in New York, first on the Lower East Side and then, in 1854, on Lispenard Street in what is now known as Tribeca. Bernard Saint-Gaudens established a shoe and boot shop, which attracted a fashionable clientele, and became active in French immigrant circles (his Gascon roots ran deep).

In many ways Saint-Gaudens's early years were unremarkable. Like other children of hardworking immigrants who strove to make their way in a new country, he grew up in humble circumstances. He attended grade school, which was to be the extent of his formal education. In the spring of 1861, when he was thirteen, he was apprenticed to a French émigré cameo cutter, Louis Avet, who had a shop on Broadway in New York's bustling retail district. From Avet he learned the exacting art of cameo polishing and cutting, in shell and in the more difficult medium of stone (see fig. 2). Cameos, both portraits and ideal subjects, were fashionable accessories and keepsakes, and the overworked Avet entrusted his young charge to carry out some of his commissions. Saint-Gaudens's youthful ambition was tested in a series of unsigned brooches, pendants, and bracelets that today may be firmly attributed to him only through provenance. His earliest identified cameo, perhaps from the first year of his apprenticeship, is a delicate shell portrait of New York lawyer John G. Tuffs (fig. 3), who had died in 1859. The cameo, which retains its original leather-bound case, is noteworthy for the challenging three-quarter pose. Avet was a demanding and temperamental taskmaster, and Saint-Gaudens described his years with him as "composing a miserable slavery."[1] In

Fig. 2 Augustus Saint-Gaudens (1848–1907) at his cameo lathe, ca. 1864–65

Fig. 1 Saint-Gaudens in his Paris studio, with a plaster cast of *The Puritan* (fig. 26), 1898

autumn 1864 he parted company with Avet and went to work for another French cameo cutter, Jules Le Brethon, also based on Broadway. Le Brethon was a far more sympathetic employer, and under his avuncular tutelage Saint-Gaudens thrived.

Like many aspiring artists who worked by day, Saint-Gaudens supplemented his training by enrolling in evening art courses. By 1864 he was attending night drawing classes at the Cooper Union on East Seventh Street, which had been established in 1859 and offered free tuition to working-class students. During the 1863–64 term he also was enrolled in antique classes at the National Academy of Design, drawing from its collection of plaster casts copied after antique statuary. In 1866 he supplemented this first step in formal studies with life classes, where he drew from human models both draped and undraped. The academy (conveniently located next to his father's shoe shop at Twenty-third Street and Fourth Avenue and not far from where the family lived at Twenty-first Street between First and Second Avenues) was the foremost institution for American art training, and during his tenure there Saint-Gaudens encountered major artists and teachers of the day, including sculptors John Quincy Adams Ward and Launt Thompson and painters Daniel Huntington (see cat. 3) and Emanuel Leutze (painter of the Metropolitan's *Washington Crossing the Delaware*).

Although in the mid-nineteenth century most major American sculptors expatriated to Italy to work in more congenial artistic surroundings, a small group of professional sculptors remained in New York. John Quincy Adams Ward (1830–1910), the so-called dean of American sculptors, was at the forefront. He and his mentor Henry Kirke Brown (1814–1886) responded to a growing call for subjects based on American themes, executed in a realistic style and in a bronze medium celebrated for its democratic overtones. Brown's *George Washington* (1851–56) for Union Square and Ward's *Indian Hunter* (1866) for Central Park anticipated the full-blown naturalism of the Beaux-Arts bronze aesthetic that would be mastered by Saint-Gaudens and his generation. (Saint-Gaudens later recalled that *The Indian Hunter* had a profound effect on him when he saw the plaster cast exhibited in 1865.) At the close of the Civil War in 1865, the demand for public monuments memorializing departed heroes resulted in no end of commissions for this growing pool of home-based talent.

In February 1867 Saint-Gaudens departed for France to continue his formal art studies. He was among the first American sculptors who opted to train in Paris rather than in Italy. For several decades Americans like Hiram Powers and William Wetmore Story had flocked to Florence and Rome for the ready availability of marble and trained craftsmen and carvers, not to mention the artistic riches and lively expatriate community. But the Neoclassical aesthetic, with its idealized forms and subject matter, offered little tangible reflection of contemporary American life, and in the 1860s the mecca of aspiring artists shifted to Paris, in particular the rigorous program of studies at the prestigious state-run École des Beaux-Arts. While Saint-Gaudens waited out the

Fig. 3 Augustus Saint-Gaudens. *John Tuffs*, ca. 1861. Shell, 1¾ x 1½ in. (4.5 x 3.8 cm). The Metropolitan Museum of Art, Purchase, Sheila W. and Richard J. Schwartz Gift and Morris K. Jesup Fund, 1990 (1990.78.1a, b) (cat. 1)

protracted process of applying to the École des Beaux-Arts through the American consulate, he enrolled at the École Gratuite de Dessin, better known as the Petite École, on the Rue de l'École de Médecine. There he took classes in sculptural composition as well as the standard antique and life drawing classes with masters Gustave-Jean Jacquet and Alexandre Laemlein.

Parisian life was both thrilling and challenging. Saint-Gaudens had deliberately timed his arrival to coincide with the 1867 Exposition Universelle, one of a series of great world's fairs that proclaimed Paris the cultural capital of the late nineteenth century. At the exhibition he saw the work of fellow up-and-coming Americans such as Winslow Homer and James A. M. Whistler and also was exposed to such leading French artists as Paul Dubois, whose sculptures would deeply influence his own developing style. Saint-Gaudens's fluency in French and his innate charisma helped smooth his transition to full-time student life. He not only socialized with fellow Americans but also developed lasting friendships with French artists. To assuage the financial privations of student life, he carved cameos for an Italian jeweler named Lupi.

After six months at the Petite École Saint-Gaudens was admitted to the atelier of the well-respected François Jouffroy (1806–1882), one of three sculpture professors at the École des Beaux Arts. In March 1868, on Jouffroy's recommendation, he finally earned formal admission to the École, located on the Rue Bonaparte across the Seine from the Louvre. As a Beaux-Arts student Saint-Gaudens gained proficiency by drawing and modeling from the nude and completing preliminary sketches that led to more polished compositions. The curriculum emphasized above all the realistic treatment of the human form, expressed in a bold, vital style. As a result of reforms instituted in 1863, all students, regardless of specialty, were drilled in the interdependence of painting, sculpture, architecture, and design in the creative process. An architect, for instance, was taught the benefits of embellishing his buildings with sculpture, while a sculptor was instructed to use a classical architectural vocabulary when designing pedestals. This osmotic approach to design informed Saint-Gaudens's approach to monument making throughout his career.

The outbreak of the Franco-Prussian War in July 1870 interrupted the pleasant routine of Saint-Gaudens's student days. In September, as the Prussian armies advanced on Paris, Saint-Gaudens left to visit his brother Andrew (1851–1891), who was working in a Limoges porcelain factory. After several months he moved on to Italy, where he discovered "a door . . . thrown wide open to the eternal beauty of the classical."[2] During his years in Rome, from 1870 to 1875 (with one return trip to New York in 1872–73), Saint-Gaudens began the transition from student to professional artist. He found a studio in the gardens of the Palazzo Barberini, in the shadows of the grand apartments of successful American expatriate sculptors William Wetmore Story and Randolph Rogers. How much contact he had with Story and Rogers has not been documented, but he did know and admire William Rinehart, a popular Baltimorean transplant who died in 1874.

Saint-Gaudens shared his Rome studio with the Portuguese sculptor António Soares dos Reis (1847–1889), who had been a fellow student at the École des Beaux-Arts. Both men set to work on ambitious full-size compositions, demonstration pieces that were intended to entice prospective patrons. For his all-American subject (fig. 4), Saint-Gaudens drew on the popular epic poem "The Song of Hiawatha" published by Henry Wadsworth Longfellow in 1855. He depicted the chief in a melancholic seated pose. With

Fig. 4 Augustus Saint-Gaudens. *Hiawatha*, 1871–72 (this carving, 1874). Marble, 60 x 34½ x 37¼ in. (152.4 x 87.6 x 94.6 cm). The Metropolitan Museum of Art, Gift of Diane, Daniel, and Mathew Wolf, in memory of Catherine Hoover Voorsanger, 2001 (2001.641) (cat. 4)

its broad planar surface treatment and narrative accoutrement, the nude figure offers a nod toward the lingering Neoclassical tradition. With youthful self-assurance Saint-Gaudens vowed that *Hiawatha* "would amaze the world and settle my future."[3] His first significant patron, attorney Montgomery Gibbs, paid to have the sculpture cast in plaster from the clay model, a critical intermediary step, and in late 1873 Saint-Gaudens received an order from Edwin D. Morgan, a former governor of New York, to have the work translated to marble. It was completed in 1874 and installed in Morgan's New York City house along with his extensive art collection.

In Rome Saint-Gaudens ingratiated himself with the lively community of Anglo-American expatriates, both at private parties and in the famous Caffè Greco on the Via dei Condotti, where an international coterie gathered. Word of Saint-Gaudens's talents spread to visiting Americans. In 1872 Hannah Rohr Tuffs requested he carve a shell cameo of herself (see cat. 2), a pendant of sorts to his earlier portrait of her late husband. (As he had in Paris, Saint-Gaudens cut cameos in Rome to supplement his income.) She also ordered a marble portrait of her sister Eva Rohr (fig. 5), an aspiring singer whom Saint-Gaudens portrayed in the guise of Marguerite in Charles Gounod's opera *Faust*. This was the sculptor's first bust commission and one of several winsome portraits of young American women that he executed in Rome.

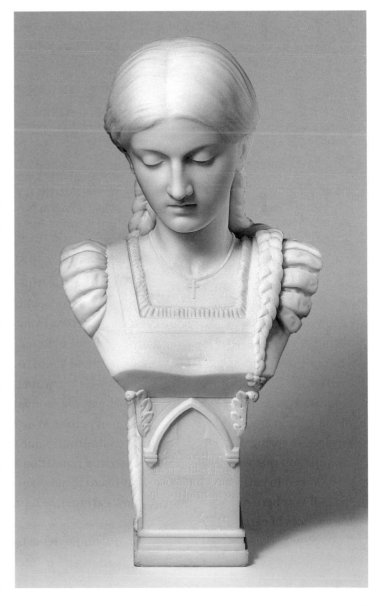

Fig. 5 Augustus Saint-Gaudens. *Eva Rohr,* 1872. Marble, 18⅝ x 9¼ x 6½ in. (47.3 x 23.5 x 16.5 cm). The Metropolitan Museum of Art, Gift of Allan H. Smith, 1990 (1990.317) (cat. 5)

Montgomery Gibbs introduced Saint-Gaudens to lawyer and politician William Maxwell Evarts (1818–1901), who was in Europe as the chief counsel for the United States on the Geneva Arbitration and who visited Rome frequently with his family. Evarts requested that Saint-Gaudens cut several marble copies after antique busts from the Vatican collections, first *Demosthenes* (fig. 6) and *Cicero* and later *Young Emperor Augustus* (now considered a portrait of Gaius, Augustus's grandson), all in the collection of Erving and Joyce Wolf. These unsigned works were representative of the type of souvenirs that cultivated Grand Tourists purchased to memorialize their visits to the Eternal City.

Evarts's pleasure with these commissions led him to order his own portrait (fig. 7), for which sittings took place in New York in 1872 (Gibbs had financed Saint-Gaudens's return). While remaining true to such classicizing portrait conventions as the ennobling herm base, Saint-Gaudens created an incisive and boldly realistic portrait of Evarts. The result, which far surpasses his other early marble portraits, is an early manifestation of his ability to penetrate and project individual character. Favorably impressed, Evarts allowed his bust to be shown in the Philadelphia Centennial International Exhibition in 1876. Saint-Gaudens was pleased with the portrait's placement in the show, but in fact it was eclipsed by hundreds of American and Italian marbles of ideal subjects, the swan song of a moribund Neoclassical style. Nevertheless, the exhibition introduced his work to a mass audience. All the while,

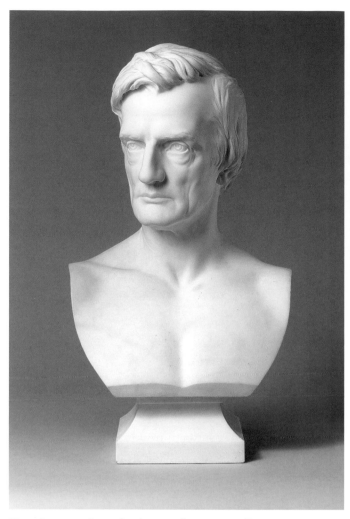

Fig. 6 Augustus Saint-Gaudens. *Demosthenes*, 1873–74. Marble, 21¾ x 11½ x 10¾ in. (55.2 x 29.2 x 27.3 cm). The Metropolitan Museum of Art, lent by Erving and Joyce Wolf, in memory of Diane R. Wolf (L.1986.112.2)

Fig. 7 Augustus Saint-Gaudens. *William Maxwell Evarts*, 1872 73 (this carving, 1874). Marble, 22⅞ x 12¾ x 9¼ in. (58.1 x 32.4 x 23.5 cm). The Metropolitan Museum of Art, Gift of Erving and Joyce Wolf, in memory of Diane R. Wolf, 1987 (1987.405) (cat. 6)

his network of American patrons grew, as the powerful and well-connected Evarts recommended him for portrait busts of other prominent clients. Several of these were modeled during Saint-Gaudens's stay in New York from the summer of 1872 to the spring of 1873 and were then translated to marble in Rome, either by the sculptor himself or by the skilled Italian carvers he now could afford to pay.

Back in Rome, in December 1873 Saint-Gaudens met the American art student Augusta Homer (1848–1926; fig. 8) of Roxbury, Massachusetts, who was from a family of old Boston stock and a distant relation of painter Winslow Homer. The couple was engaged in spring 1874 but delayed the wedding until Saint-Gaudens could earn a major commission that would broaden his American reputation and enable him to support a wife. When in early 1875 Saint-Gaudens heard about plans for a New York monument to Civil War hero Admiral David Glasgow Farragut, he returned to America to improve his chances of earning the commission.

In New York, Saint-Gaudens settled in a studio in the German Savings Bank building at Fourth Avenue and Fourteenth Street, where painter and stained glass designer David Maitland Armstrong, a friend from Rome, also worked. Saint-Gaudens later

Fig. 8 Augusta Homer, 1874

described these times as "the usual hard ones of artists' beginnings," acknowledging that he had to "be content to labor for reputation."[4] Creatively, however, he flourished. Not only was he talented, but he possessed an abundance of charm and an intrinsic gift for friendship that reaped him enormous professional benefits. Soon he was immersed in a ferment of young artistic talent, and within months of his return he had met painter-decorator John La Farge (1835–1910) and architects Stanford White (1853–1906) and Charles Follen McKim (1847–1909).

Saint-Gaudens also befriended genteel New Yorker Richard Watson Gilder (1844–1909; see cat. 11). The multitalented Gilder was a poet, an activist, and a journalist for *Scribner's Monthly,* and when *Scribner's* became *Century Illustrated Monthly Magazine* in 1881 he took the reins as its editor. Gilder was Saint-Gaudens's greatest trumpeter. With other like-minded writers he professed him a leader in a new movement of American sculptors who were rigorously trained in Parisian academies but returned home to practice their art. Saint-Gaudens eagerly accepted these men's tutelage in the social and professional rituals of courting clients and establishing a foothold in New York's rapidly growing art world. (His brother Louis observed that by the end of his career Saint-Gaudens could "curry favor with the rich like a flunkey."[5])

While he was busy wooing members of the New York Farragut Monument Committee Saint-Gaudens completed very little new independent sculpture, but he did take on a range of collaborative projects to provide steady income. He modeled elements for several pieces of presentation silver for Tiffany & Co., among them an ornate vase (fig. 9) that was a gift to poet and publisher William Cullen Bryant. Following the designs of James H. Whitehouse, Saint-Gaudens modeled at least five of the six relief medallions for the upper portion of the vase, one a portrait of Bryant, three that depict incidents in his life, and two allegorical scenes.

From time to time Saint-Gaudens based himself in Boston to be near Augusta Homer and her family. Between November 1876 and February 1877, despite scant experience as a painter, he worked under John La Farge's direction painting murals for the sanctuary of Henry Hobson Richardson's Trinity Church (consecrated in 1877) on Copley Square. His figures of Saints Paul and James, executed after La Farge's designs, stand alongside contributions by Francis Davis Millet (see cat. 10) and others who worked in this Renaissance-style workshop and became lifelong friends and professional colleagues. Over the next few years Saint-Gaudens became La Farge's sculptor-collaborator of choice: he modeled and translated into marble La Farge's design for the Edward King family tomb in Island Cemetery in Newport, Rhode Island (1877–78); produced chancel reredos (high-relief altar panels) for Saint Thomas Church in New York (1877; destroyed 1905); and executed sculptural

Fig. 9 Designed by James Horton Whitehouse (1833–1922); manufactured by Tiffany & Co. (founded 1837); at least five of the six medallions on the body modeled by Augustus Saint-Gaudens; chased by Eugene J. Soligny (1833–1901). *The Bryant Vase,* 1875–76. Silver; 33½ x 14 x 11¼ in. (85.1 x 35.6 x 28.7 cm), diam. 11¼ in. (28.7 cm), 452 oz. 16 dwt. (14084.2 g). The Metropolitan Museum of Art, Gift of William Cullen Bryant, 1877 (77.9a, b) (cat. 7)

decorations for the ornate interior program of the Cornelius Vanderbilt II mansion in New York (1881–83; see fig. 16, cats. 18, 19).

The Farragut Monument was the most sought-after commission by sculptors of the day. David Glasgow Farragut (1801–1870) was the most celebrated naval hero of the Civil War, best known for his capture of New Orleans in 1862 and his victory in the Battle of Mobile Bay in 1864, when he issued his famous command, "Damn the torpedoes! Full speed ahead!" He was named the nation's first full admiral in 1866. For the honor of modeling his monument Saint-Gaudens pursued a calculated course of lobbying. His contacts with such patrons as Gibbs, Evarts, and Morgan earned him access to members of the Farragut Monument Committee and the Farragut family. In spite of his dogged efforts, which even extended to borrowing photographs of the admiral to prepare a plaster head study, Saint-Gaudens lost the prized commission to John Quincy Adams Ward by a margin of six votes to five. Ward, however, was overburdened with other orders for monuments and generously relinquished the commission in favor of the young, untested Saint-Gaudens, who earned it officially in December 1876.

With the order for the Farragut Monument secure, Saint-Gaudens married Augusta Homer on June 4, 1877. Two days later the couple embarked for Paris, which the sculptor felt would be the most hospitable working environment for the creation of the Farragut and three other recently garnered commissions. New York may have been an up-and-coming center for art, but Paris was its world capital, with access to sculptural models and materials, experienced bronze technicians, and a thriving international fraternity of artists. Saint-Gaudens's time in Paris (see fig. 10)—until mid-1880 with a brief interlude in Rome in winter 1877–78—was principally occupied with composing and endlessly reworking the Farragut model, to the point where he confessed that "all my brain can conceive of now is arms with braid, legs, coats, eagles, caps, legs, arms, hands, caps, eagles, eagles, caps and so on; nothing, nothing but that statue."[6] His study for the head of Farragut (cat. 13) presages the final result (see fig. 14), in which the stalwart admiral bears a furrowed brow and resolute expression. Soon after Saint-Gaudens received the commission, Stanford White offered to help design the pedestal, and the sculptor quickly agreed. White arrived in Paris in summer 1878, and during his year abroad the two men embarked on an intense and inspired collaboration on the base of the monument.

For Saint-Gaudens his halcyon years in Paris were a "marked turning-point in [his] life."[7] He became a central figure in the expatriate American artistic circles, and his studio on the Rue Notre Dame des Champs was a popular gathering place. In 1877 in New York he had been a cofounder of the progressive Society of American Artists, an alternative exhibition venue to the established National Academy of Design; in Paris he lobbied cosmopolitan expatriate artists to send their works to New York for the society's first exhibition. In 1878, after a winter in Rome, Saint-Gaudens gained additional exposure among American artists when he joined Maitland Armstrong on the American jury of selection for the Exposition Universelle. They vetted and hung American paintings, watercolors, and drawings, favoring the works of younger artists like Winslow Homer, Mary Cassatt, and John Singer Sargent who adopted a poetic, looser painting style over the transcriptional one favored by landscape painters of the Hudson River School. The Paris years introduced Saint-Gaudens to lifelong artistic confreres such as George de Forest Brush, Kenyon Cox, and Sargent (see cat. 14). The sculptor

Fig. 10 Saint-Gaudens in Paris, 1878

also cemented enduring personal and professional bonds with Stanford White and Charles McKim when the three redheads took a walking tour in southern France during the summer of 1878, the year before the architectural firm of McKim, Mead & White was established (see cat. 8).

These jovial relationships spawned a series of some twenty small relief portraits that are as innovative as they are charming. Secure with income from the Farragut Monument, Saint-Gaudens modeled these portraits, first in New York and later in Paris, as outright gifts of friendship or in exchange for a work of art by the sitter. Even the few that were commissioned evince a similar freedom of aesthetic. For this series, Saint-Gaudens took as his inspiration reliefs by contemporary French sculptor Henri Chapu and, especially, the quattrocento medallions of Antonio Pisano (Pisanello), plaster casts of which Saint-Gaudens displayed in his studio. Most of these reliefs are shoulder-length profile portraits set on vertical undulating supports. As pictorial as they are sculptural, they were novel for their sketchy handling of form that melds with the background, a technique considered "unfinished" in academic circles. Saint-Gaudens also included attributes to individualize the sitters, such as classicizing acanthus leaves for architect McKim (fig. 11) and a palette and brushes for painters Frank Millet (see cat. 10) and Jules Bastien-Lepage (fig. 12). The distinctive inscriptions, rendered in

Fig. 12 Augustus Saint-Gaudens. *Jules Bastien-Lepage*, 1880 (this cast, 1910). Bronze, 14¾ x 10½ in. (37.5 x 26.7 cm). The Metropolitan Museum of Art, Gift by subscription through the Saint-Gaudens Memorial Committee, 1912 (12.76.4) (cat. 15)

Fig. 11 Augustus Saint-Gaudens. *Charles F. McKim*, 1878. Bronze, 7⅜ x 4⅞ in. (18.7 x 12.4 cm). The Metropolitan Museum of Art, Gift of Mrs. Charles D. Norton, 1924 (24.20) (cat. 9)

Fig. 13 Augustus Saint-Gaudens. *Richard Watson Gilder, Helena de Kay Gilder, and Rodman de Kay Gilder*, 1879 (this cast, ca. 1883–84). Plaster, 8⅝ x 16⅞ in. (21.9 x 42.9 cm). The Metropolitan Museum of Art, Gift of David and Joshua Gilder, 2002 (2002.445) (cat. 11)

Saint-Gaudens's characteristic Roman-style lettering punctuated by bullets, are affectionate tributes to his sitters and vital elements in the overall composition. On McKim's relief, for instance, he inscribed "in souvenir of the ten jolly days passed with you and the illustrious Stanford White in the south of France." These compact reliefs not only deftly record the sitters' physical appearance but also project psychological impressions of them.

At this time Saint-Gaudens also began excerpting elements from his finished sculptures to create distinct new compositions, a practice he continued throughout the rest of his career. His first multifigure portrait, of Richard Watson Gilder, Helena de Kay Gilder, and young Rodman de Kay Gilder (fig. 13) was modeled when the family visited Paris in spring 1879. It spawned the more detailed single portrait of Rodman (see cat. 12) floating on an etched field of bronze. Such "recycling" of his sculptures allowed Saint-Gaudens to further experiment with and refine his compositions, and it also increased his commercial and critical exposure. He exhibited many of these smaller works at American venues, notably the Society of American Artists, during the career-building 1870s and 1880s. Although they have been eclipsed by his most successful monuments, their regular public display was integral to the development of his reputation and allowed his art to be measured directly against that of other sculptors.

One significant and symbolic indication of an artist's professional coming of age in the nineteenth century was having work accepted for the annual Paris Salon, the premier forum for the exhibition, reception, and sale of paintings and sculpture. For Saint-Gaudens, this moment came in spring 1880 with the submission of the full-size plaster model of the Farragut Monument and five bas-relief portraits. Although he was disappointed with the installation of the Farragut sculpture at the Salon (it was at first placed under a balcony), he gained important critical feedback prior to the casting of the monument in permanent bronze in the Parisian foundry Gruet Jeune in June (the first pouring had proved a failure). He earned an honorable mention for his entries in the Salon, the first American sculptor to be accorded that distinction.

In July 1880, after the Farragut Monument was successfully cast, Saint-Gaudens and his pregnant wife returned to New York. In September she gave birth to their only child, Homer (1880–1958). Saint-Gaudens leased a studio at the Sherwood Studio Building at Sixth Avenue and Fifty-seventh Street, which had just been completed in 1880 and was attracting a number of recently returned foreign-trained artists. His apartment-studio at the Sherwood was not entirely suitable for a sculptor, however, especially one who relished his privacy, as the workspace was too small and had no ground-floor access. Within months, Saint-Gaudens decamped to 148 West Thirty-sixth Street, which would serve as his primary studio for the next sixteen years (along with other additional rented spaces). During the 1880s he lived at 22 Washington Place, just off Washington Square, and from 1890 until 1897, at 51 West Forty-fifth Street.

The unveiling of the Farragut Monument (fig. 14) on May 25, 1881, in Madison Square Park was seen from the start as a remarkable turning point in the history of

Fig. 14 Augustus Saint-Gaudens; base designed by Augustus Saint-Gaudens and Stanford White. Farragut Monument, Madison Square Park, New York, 1877–80. Bronze

American public sculpture, and rightly so. The figure of Farragut, while thoroughly modern in modeling and uniform, distinctly evokes the Italian Renaissance masters Saint-Gaudens so revered. He professed great admiration for Pisanello, Verrocchio, and Ghiberti, and the Farragut Monument freely references the pose of Donatello's *Saint George* (1415–17) in the Bargello in Florence. But Saint-Gaudens also broke new ground with his energetic Beaux-Arts figure, a highly naturalistic treatment of form energized by the richly textured surface and spirited play of light on volume and void. And he infused the combination of Italian Renaissance principles and French training with dashes of American modernity—creating a fluid dynamic between tradition and innovation that echoed the overall leitmotif of American Renaissance aesthetics.

The bronze admiral stands upon an unusual high-backed exedra, or bench, with a raised central pier and semicircular flanking wings. (The deteriorating Hudson River bluestone base was replaced by a black granite copy in 1935; the original is at the Saint-Gaudens National Historic Site in Cornish, New Hampshire.) White and Saint-Gaudens's design for the base was a significant departure from a traditional unadorned stone shaft. The horizontal "stage" presents the coolly alert Farragut as if he were standing windblown on the prow of a ship scanning the seas, his spyglass in his left hand and his sword at his side. Two allegorical females, Courage and Loyalty, sit amid stylized waves and a decorative inscription that celebrates Farragut's accomplishments. The ends are capped with low-relief dolphins, again suggestive of Farragut's marine domain.

Novel too was the way Saint-Gaudens and White set the monument within its landscaped environment, in a dialogue with the surrounding buildings, trees, shrubs, walkways, and other sculptures in Madison Square Park. When spectators approached the statue in its original location (the northwest corner of the park at Fifth Avenue and Twenty-sixth Street), they mounted a set of low steps that led to an intimate pebble-paved raised platform. Whether they stood at the admiral's feet or sat on the bench, they were meant to be stirred by this exemplar of modern heroism and patriotism. Like the best American commemorative civic sculpture of the era, the Farragut Monument aimed to reform, to moralize, and to teach standards of beauty.

Fig. 16 Augustus Saint-Gaudens. Mantelpiece from the Cornelius Vanderbilt II House, New York, ca. 1881–83. Marble, mosaic, oak, cast iron; 15 ft. 4⅜ in. x 12 ft. 10⅞ in. x 3 ft. 1¼ in. (4.7 x 3.9 x 1 m). The Metropolitan Museum of Art, Gift of Mrs. Cornelius Vanderbilt II, 1925 (25.234) (cat. 18)

The uniformly favorable critical response to the Farragut Monument assured Saint-Gaudens's success as a professional sculptor and a cultural role model. Critics recognized the thirty-three-year-old as the new face of American sculpture, the instigator of a movement by French-trained sculptors to import cosmopolitan training and integrate it with real-life American subject matter that paralleled an analogous movement in American painting in the 1880s and 1890s by the likes of Childe Hassam, Theodore Robinson, and J. Alden Weir. Saint-Gaudens's studio grew to the point that he took on assistants, among them Frederick William MacMonnies (1863–1937), who rose from tending clay to become his protégé, and his younger brother Louis St. Gaudens (1854–1913; he preferred an abbreviated version of the family surname). With his workshop system, Saint-Gaudens was able to carry out numerous commissions simultaneously. His French friend Paul Bion appropriately described him in 1881 as "drowning in work, . . . a sort of 'Edisson' of sculpture, combining, constructing, producing treasure on treasure."[8]

The 1880s represented a coming of age for an elite class of newly moneyed New Yorkers who had made their millions as a result of the country's rapid industrialization and developments in transportation and communications. During the Gilded Age (so named by Mark Twain and Charles Dudley Warner in their eponymous 1873 book), the demand for luxurious goods and imposing mansions was met by an ambitious group of architects, painters, sculptors, and decorators who believed that these collaborative projects stood as powerful reflections of their county's growing cultural presence on the world stage as it assumed its rightful place in a distinguished artistic continuum. These symbiotic partnerships inspired some of the most remarkable products of the American Renaissance, a period of unprecedented artistic cross-fertilization that began in the mid-1870s and continued through the 1910s.

Saint-Gaudens was involved in several ambitious residential projects. Between 1880 and 1883 he was hired by the architect George Browne Post to produce sculpture for the palatial French Renaissance–style Cornelius Vanderbilt II house on Fifth Avenue at Fifty-seventh Street (demolished 1925–27). Post had contracted with John La Farge for a sumptuous interior program budgeted at $100,000, with La Farge directing the overall project and also contributing individual elements such as stained glass (see fig. 15). For his most extensive foray into collaborative interior work, Saint-Gaudens was called upon to execute the monumental marble mantel for the entrance hall, which features two caryatids, Amor and Pax, supporting the mosaic overmantel (fig. 16). With the help of his brother Louis, MacMonnies, and other assistants, Saint-Gaudens completed not only the elaborate mantel but fourteen carved and inlaid wood panels for the dining room ceiling as well (see cat. 19). In 1882 he also modeled three rectangular bas-relief portraits of family members, his most decoratively treated to date: "Commodore" Cornelius Vanderbilt I (fig. 17), William Henry II and Cornelius Vanderbilt III, and Gertrude Vanderbilt, who would later become a sculptor and who founded the Whitney Museum of American Art in New York in 1931 (plaster versions are at the Saint-Gaudens National Historic Site, Cornish, New Hampshire).

While Saint-Gaudens was garnering lucrative monumental commissions, he continued to produce bas-reliefs, some for love, others for money. Of the former ilk is an intimate portrait of his two-year-old son Homer seated in a child-size chair, his pudgy hand gripping its arm (fig. 18). Most of the reliefs he made, however, were commissioned,

Fig. 17 Augustus Saint-Gaudens. *Cornelius Vanderbilt I*, 1882. Bronze, 16¼ x 22¾ in. (41.3 x 57.8 cm). Heirs of Countess László Széchenyi

Fig. 18 Augustus Saint-Gaudens. *Homer Schiff Saint-Gaudens*, 1882 (this carving, 1906–7). Marble, 20¼ x 10⅜ in. (51.4 x 26.4 cm). The Metropolitan Museum of Art, Gift of Jacob H. Schiff, 1905 (05.15.2) (cat. 20)

Fig. 19 Augustus Saint-Gaudens. *Samuel Gray Ward*, 1881 (this cast, 1908). Bronze, 19 x 13¾ in. (48.3 x 34.9 cm). The Metropolitan Museum of Art, Gift of Mrs. Augustus Saint-Gaudens, 1912 (12.29) (cat. 17)

Fig. 20 Augustus Saint-Gaudens. *The Children of Jacob H. Schiff*, 1884–85 (this carving, 1906–7). Marble, 68⅞ x 51 in. (174.9 x 129.5 cm). The Metropolitan Museum of Art, Gift of Jacob H. Schiff, 1905 (05.15.3) (cat. 23)

reflecting the escalating demand for his work. The early bas-reliefs, from the late 1870s, are cabinet-size; many of the later ones are significantly larger. One of his own particular favorites was the half-length relief of Samuel Gray Ward (fig. 19) he executed in 1881 in the sketchy style he had perfected in earlier portraits, a virtuoso exercise in which the sculptor's clay approaches fluid pigment, especially in the textured cloth of the jacket and the bristly beard and moustache. The appealing full-length portrait he made in 1884–85 of the children of Jacob H. Schiff posed in an architectural framework with a garland-festooned cornice and slender pilasters (fig. 20) is more ambitious, not only in composition but also in the extent of finish and the varying degrees of relief. Saint-Gaudens completed more than eighty of these bas-relief sculptures. In the words of his genial competitor (and Metropolitan Museum trustee) Daniel Chester French, he "established a precedent for an attractive form of the art that bids fair to be followed (probably at a respectful distance) for all time."[9]

In summer 1883 Saint-Gaudens traveled west with Stanford White first to the New Mexico Territory and then on to Los Angeles, San Francisco, and Portland. He returned via Chicago, where he met with local dignitaries about a proposed statue of Abraham Lincoln for Lincoln Park to be funded by the estate of lumber merchant Eli Bates. Since 1875, when he entered an unfairly juried competition for a monument to Senator Charles Sumner in Boston, Saint-Gaudens had refused to compete against other sculptors for commissions. Instead he courted committee members, relying on his established reputation, not to mention his considerable charm, to earn orders. After holding a competition that attracted four unsatisfactory proposals by other sculptors, in 1883 the Chicago Lincoln Memorial Fund awarded him a commission for the Lincoln statue and also for the Eli Bates Fountain, *Storks at Play* (which he modeled in collaboration with MacMonnies and which was installed in Lincoln Park in 1886–87).

The honor of sculpting a portrait of Lincoln particularly resonated with Saint-Gaudens. In February 1861, when he was almost thirteen years old, he had seen the president-elect in New York. Four years later, after Lincoln's assassination on April 14, 1865, Saint-Gaudens joined thousands at City Hall to pay his respects to the slain president. He recalled that

> after joining the interminable line that formed somewhere down Chatham Street and led up by the bier at the head of the staircase, I saw Lincoln lying in state . . . , and I went back to the end of the line to look at him again. This completed my vision of the big man, though the funeral, which I viewed from the roof of the old Wallack's Theater on Broome Street, deepened the profound solemnity of my impression.[10]

These youthful remembrances informed Saint-Gaudens's visions for his statue of the Great Emancipator, as did reading Lincoln's speeches and writings. (The final sentence of Lincoln's Cooper Union speech—"Let us have faith that right makes might . . . "— and phrases from the last paragraph of his second inaugural address—"With malice toward none, with charity for all . . ."—are carved on the back of the exedra in the base of the monument.) By chance, Saint-Gaudens had the good fortune of accessing the original plaster life mask and casts of the hands of Lincoln, taken by the Chicago sculptor Leonard Wells Volk in 1860. Saint-Gaudens, with Richard Watson Gilder and collectors Thomas B. Clarke and Erwin Davis, purchased the casts to present to the U.S.

Fig. 21 Louis St. Gaudens; Frederick MacMonnies; and Homer, Augusta, and Augustus Saint-Gaudens in Cornish, New Hampshire, summer 1885

Fig. 22 Augustus, Marie (his niece), and Homer Saint-Gaudens and Homer's pet goat Seasick by the Pan pool, Cornish, New Hampshire, July 1894

government. To fund the donation in 1886 they offered bronze or plaster sets of the mask and hands (cats. 25, 26) to subscribers, who eventually numbered thirty-three. Saint-Gaudens added dedicatory inscriptions to the casts in his distinctive lettering style and also oversaw casting of the bronzes at the major New York foundry of the day, Henry Bonnard Bronze Company (where his Lincoln monument would also be cast). These first-generation sets, and later casts of lesser quality, have served as valuable references for many of the sculptors who have represented Lincoln.

Fig. 23 Saint-Gaudens in his Cornish, New Hampshire, studio with the completed clay model of the *Standing Lincoln*, 1887

In 1885, eager to escape another hot New York summer, Saint-Gaudens was enticed to Cornish, New Hampshire, with the promise that he would find "plenty of Lincoln-shaped men up there."[11] In farming country overlooking the Connecticut River, Cornish boasts spectacular views of Mount Ascutney in nearby Vermont. During the summers from 1885 until 1897 (with the exception of 1889, when he visited Paris to see the Exposition Universelle), Saint-Gaudens, his family, and a cadre of assistants lived and worked in Cornish in a house (formerly a tavern) and studio (a big barn) that he rented from New York lawyer Charles Cotesworth Beaman, who was William Maxwell Evarts's son-in-law (see figs. 21, 22). In 1891 Saint-Gaudens purchased the property from Beaman and named it Aspet, after the town in the French Pyrenees where his father was born. First as a summer colony and later as a year-round haven for some (dubbed "the chickadees"), Cornish attracted a lively group of creative artists, among them painters Thomas Wilmer Dewing, George de Forest Brush, and Maxfield Parrish; architect Charles Platt; and sculptors Herbert Adams and, briefly, Daniel Chester French. Landscape designers, musicians, playwrights, and actors also comprised the thriving nexus that soon became known as the Cornish Colony.

The dramatic landscape and reflective surroundings inspired great productivity, and the social gatherings were filled with spirited discourse on the arts.

That first summer in Cornish Saint-Gaudens created numerous sketches for his *Lincoln* using a lanky six-foot-four local farmer named Langdon Morse as his model. In the final concept (figs. 23, 24), Saint-Gaudens represented a pensive Lincoln, his head lowered and his left foot slightly advanced, rising from the Chair of State as if poised to deliver an oration, a transitional moment of action and imminence. Like the Farragut Monument, Saint-Gaudens's eleven-and-a-half-foot-high statue of Lincoln was one element in a carefully planned sculptural program that encompassed the approach to the monument, its architectural setting, and nearby landscape elements. Stanford White planned the sweeping sixty-foot semicircular exedra that surrounds the central granite pedestal. The expansive viewing terrace is accessed by low curving steps that invite visitors to enter and experience the monument as if they were members of Lincoln's audience.

Fig. 24 Augustus Saint-Gaudens; architectural setting designed by Stanford White. *Abraham Lincoln: The Man*, or *Standing Lincoln*, Lincoln Park, Chicago, 1884–87. Bronze

23

Abraham Lincoln's grandson and namesake unveiled the flag-draped *Abraham Lincoln: The Man*, or *Standing Lincoln*, as it is familiarly known, on October 22, 1887, before 10,000 people. The statue was rightly seen as Saint-Gaudens's first major effort since the Farragut Monument, and it validated his reputation as a sculptor of historical figures. He was again rewarded with a positive response from the national press, both for the veracity of the likeness (see fig. 25) and for the sensitive rendering of a martyred president. Critics particularly saluted his ability to penetrate Lincoln's character, to capture, as the *Chicago Tribune* put it, "simple, lofty, strong, kind, but plain, honest, rugged, Lincoln."[12]

Saint-Gaudens's thematic range was further proven by the unveiling of *The Puritan* (fig. 26) in Springfield, Massachusetts, on Thanksgiving Day, 1887, just a month after the *Standing Lincoln*. Public monuments celebrating pilgrim heroes were commissioned by modern-day patrons in the late nineteenth century as links to distinguished ancestral lineages. Commissioned in 1881 by the Chapin family, *The Puritan* celebrates their ancestor Deacon Samuel Chapin (1598–1675), one of the original settlers of Springfield. Saint-Gaudens faced a challenge: with no individual portrait of Chapin to refer to, by necessity he produced an imagined likeness. Although he informed his depiction by looking at seventeenth-century woodcuts for costume and studying the features of Chapin's descendents, it projects not accurate physiognomy but rather the quintessential historical ideals associated with seventeenth-century pilgrims to the New World—stalwartness, uprightness, and religious fervor.

*The Puritan* represents Chapin striding determinedly forward through the New England wilderness, suggested by the scattered pine branches on the base. Enveloped in a great cloak, his face sternly shadowed by a broad-brimmed steeple hat, the stolid figure holds a heavy volume—undoubtedly a Bible—with his left arm and a sturdy walking stick in his right hand. *The Puritan* represented another successful monumental collaboration between Saint-Gaudens and White. White planned the long axis of the original site in Stearns Square to feature the statue at one end and a fountain with a central orb and four bronze turtles piped to spout water at the other end. His preliminary sketch for the site (fig. 27) reveals plans for an allée of birch trees and a high hedge behind the statue. As have the sites of nearly all of Saint-Gaudens's major monuments, the original setting of *The Puritan* has been compromised. The sculpture, with no other accoutrement save White's stepped circular granite base, was relocated to nearby Merrick Park in 1899.

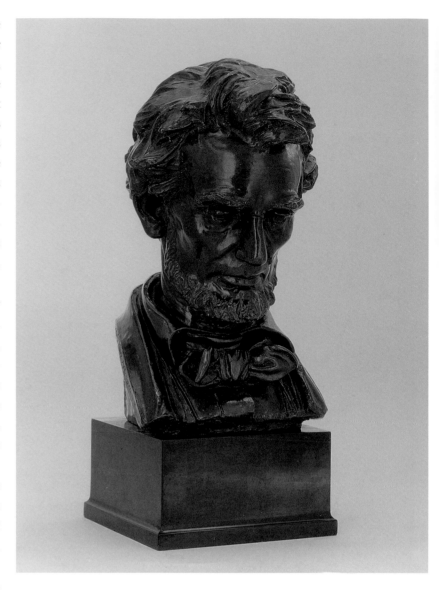

Fig. 25 Augustus Saint-Gaudens. *Head of Lincoln*, 1887 (this cast, after 1907). Bronze, 16½ x 11 x 11½ in. (41.9 x 27.9 x 29.2 cm). United States Department of the Interior, National Park Service, Saint-Gaudens National Historic Site, Cornish, New Hampshire

Fig. 26 Augustus Saint-Gaudens; base designed by Stanford White. *The Puritan (Deacon Samuel Chapin)*, Merrick Park, Springfield, Massachusetts, 1883–86. Bronze

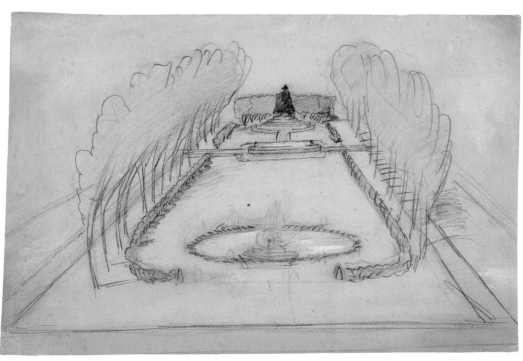

Fig. 27 Stanford White (1853–1906). *Sketch of Saint-Gaudens's Statue of Deacon Samuel Chapin, Springfield, Massachusetts*, ca. 1887. Pastel, charcoal, and pencil on paper; 12 x 18⅛ in. (30.5 x 46 cm). The Metropolitan Museum of Art, Morris K. Jesup Fund, 1999 (1999.249) (cat. 28)

Fig. 28 A concert in Saint-Gaudens's studio at 148 West Thirty-sixth Street, New York. As the handwritten inscriptions record, among the audience members were painter Kenyon Cox, journalist Richard Watson Gilder, literature professor Brander Matthews, Saint-Gaudens, and architect Stanford White.

By the mid-1880s, his career firmly established, Saint-Gaudens had become an active participant in New York's blossoming cultural community. While he was never a "club-man" per se, he became a member of the Century Association in 1886 and of the Players Club (for actors, artists, and literati), his favorite, in 1888. His Thirty-sixth Street studio was a gathering place for the young cultural elite, especially for his popular Sunday afternoon concerts, the result of Saint-Gaudens's lifelong love of music (see fig. 28). As the anointed leading American sculptor of the new generation, Saint-Gaudens felt a responsibility to "give back," not only by mentoring his studio assistants but also by teaching. Many artists who worked in Saint-Gaudens's studio, such as MacMonnies, Alexander Phimister Proctor, Adolph Alexander Weinman, and James Earle Fraser (all represented in the Metropolitan's collections), went on to have highly successful careers as independent sculptors. Beginning in 1888 Saint-Gaudens taught at the Art Students League (see fig. 29) in the company of such other well-known artist-teachers as William Merritt Chase and Kenyon Cox. He continued to teach modeling classes there until his departure for Paris in 1897.

Fig. 29 Saint-Gaudens with a modeling class at the Art Students League, New York, ca. 1888

Saint-Gaudens's creative energy was dedicated principally to monumental work during the 1880s, but he also produced a series of stellar portrait reliefs. His portrait of Bessie Springs Smith White in her wedding gown and long veil (cat. 22) was his gift to Stanford White and his bride upon their marriage in 1884. Later translated to marble (fig. 30), the relief was enhanced by an elaborate Renaissance Revival gilded wood frame of White's design. Saint-Gaudens's admiration for the sitters inspired other reliefs from this period: an elegant vertical portrait of steadfastly loyal critic and author Mariana Van Rensselaer, again in a

26

Fig. 30 Augustus Saint-Gaudens. *Mrs. Stanford White (Bessie Springs Smith)*, 1884 (this carving, by 1888). Marble; 25 x 12 in. (63.5 x 30.5 cm), with frame 39½ x 24 in. (100.3 x 61 cm). The Metropolitan Museum of Art, Gift of Erving Wolf Foundation, in memory of Diane R. Wolf, 1976 (1976.388) (cat. 21)

White-designed frame (fig. 31), and a likeness of young Mrs. Grover Cleveland (Frances Folsom), started during an 1887 visit to their mutual friends, the Richard Watson Gilders, in Marion, Massachusetts (cat. 31, and see fig. 32). Saint-Gaudens's portrait of William Merritt Chase from 1888 (fig. 33) is both a sophisticated and an affectionate rendering of one of New York's most carefully crafted artistic personas. Wearing an artist's smock and a tam-o'-shanter, with brushes, maulstick, and palette in hand, Chase works energetically on a canvas beyond the portrait's edge.

Saint-Gaudens was not prone to hero worship, but he fell under the spell of Scottish author Robert Louis Stevenson (1850–1894). Having read Stevenson's *New Arabian*

Fig. 31 Augustus Saint-Gaudens. *Mrs. Schuyler Van Rensselaer (Mariana Griswold)*, 1888 (this cast, 1890). Bronze; 20⅜ x 7¾ in. (51.8 x 19.7 cm), with frame 34¾ x 16½ in. (88.3 x 41.9 cm). The Metropolitan Museum of Art, Gift of Mrs. Schuyler Van Rensselaer, 1917 (17.104) (cat. 33)

Fig. 32 Saint-Gaudens modeling his portrait of Frances Folsom Cleveland in the Gilders' studio in Marion, Massachusetts, 1887

*Nights* (1882), Saint-Gaudens told their mutual friend the artist Will H. Low that he would be privileged to meet Stevenson and to model his portrait should he travel to the United States. In autumn 1887 Stevenson arrived in New York and took rooms at the Hotel Albert on East Eleventh Street. During sittings in the company of Low and Stevenson's wife, Fanny, Saint-Gaudens devoted great effort to the portrait (fig. 34) and to settling on the perfect pose. After more sittings the following summer in Manasquan, New Jersey, Saint-Gaudens hit upon the solution of representing the tubercular Stevenson reclining in bed against pillows, with a cigarette in his hand and a sheaf of papers on his lap. The portrait of Stevenson, replicated in circular and rectangular formats and in varying dimensions, was Saint-Gaudens's most commercially successful relief.

Through John La Farge, in 1886 Saint-Gaudens received a commission from the historian Henry Adams to produce a grave monument for his wife, Marian Hooper

Fig. 33 Augustus Saint-Gaudens. *William Merritt Chase*, 1888. Bronze, 21⅝ x 29½ in. (54.9 x 74.9 cm). Collection of the American Academy of Arts and Letters, New York

Fig. 34 Augustus Saint-Gaudens. *Robert Louis Stevenson*, 1887–88 (this cast, 1910). Bronze, diam. 35¼ in. (89.5 cm). The Metropolitan Museum of Art, Gift by subscription through the Saint-Gaudens Memorial Committee, 1912 (12.76.1) (cat. 29)

Adams, who had taken her own life in 1885. Faced with the quandary of how to commemorate a suicide, Saint-Gaudens created a heavily shrouded seated figure of indeterminate gender and impenetrable mood (fig. 35). He was guided by Adams's suggestions, mediated through La Farge, that he study both Eastern and Western sources, from Buddhist statues evoking the principle of Nirvana (which Adams encountered on an 1886 trip to Japan with La Farge) to Michelangelo's sibyls in the Vatican's Sistine Chapel. The Adams figure has a raised right arm within the cloak's hood, but is otherwise devoid of action, still of emotional response. This most personal of monuments remains enigmatic, evading narrative interpretation, as patron and artist intended. Perhaps it is meant as a meditation on the inevitability and acceptance of death; in essence, one man's personal monument (which he privately referred to as "The Peace of God") has the potential to carry individual meaning or symbolism for every visitor.

The Adams Memorial was installed in 1891 in Rock Creek Cemetery in Washington, D.C. (Adams was later buried there as well.) Since the monument was designed for private rather than public contemplation, Stanford White created a peaceful and intimate space with a high-backed plinth for the sculpture, a long granite bench facing it, and a pebbled terrace. The surrounding trees and hedges created an outdoor chapel of sorts (the memorial has been relandscaped).

Fig. 35 Augustus Saint-Gaudens; architectural setting designed by Stanford White. Adams Memorial, Rock Creek Cemetery, Washington, D.C., 1886–91. Bronze

Fig. 36 "The Use and Abuse of Precedent,"
*Architectural Review* 2 (April 3, 1893), p. 21

## The Use and Abuse of Precedent.

### SECOND ARTICLE.

In a previous article, in considering the use that has been made of precedent, examples were cited in which a whole design or its main motive has been borrowed with but unimportant modifications, and in buildings intended to meet wants very different from those of the original structures, the form being thus made to do duty its original designer never dreamt of. In so far as the uses of the modern building and its prototype differ, and in so far as the original designer was successful in producing a design that was fitting and expressive, it is obvious that the borrowed form must be to that extent inappropriate and inexpressive in its new place. Its use is, therefore, to be regretted as inducing false standards of taste, however ready one may be to admit that it is better to borrow a good design than originate a bad one. If the case were one in which the new building was identical with its prototype, or nearly so, in use and position, the borrowing might be justifiable, might be the best thing that could be done. But as a matter of fact, such cases rarely, if ever, occur. Except possibly, with some of the simpler buildings, conditions never precisely repeat themselves.

The case is somewhat different with regard to the separate features of buildings. The more or less close copying of such single features, if judiciously done, may be justifiable, since their purpose is apt to be constant. Nor is it an entirely easy thing thus to use a single feature from a much-admired building and make it harmonize perfectly with its new surroundings. To do it successfully requires a thorough knowledge of the style, complete familiarity with its conditions, and a sensitive feeling for harmony. Without these qualifications on the part of the designer, the borrowed feature is sure to look like a patch. In such a case complete success is the sufficient and only justification, and it will generally be found that, where complete success has been attained, the borrowed feature has been subject to some modification more or less marked.

GIRALDA TOWER, SEVILLE.

*Copyright, 1893, by Bates, Kimball & Guild.*

MADISON SQUARE GARDEN TOWER.

At the same time he was working on the Adams Memorial, Saint-Gaudens embarked on his most public monument, *Diana the Huntress*, for Madison Square Garden. In 1887 McKim, Mead & White received a commission for a new Madison Square Garden, to be located at Madison Avenue and Twenty-sixth Street. New York's main sporting and leisure grounds, the complex would eventually boast a concert hall for 1,500, an auditorium with seating for 8,000, New York's largest restaurant, and the infamous roof garden café where Stanford White was murdered in 1906. White planned a thirty-two-story tower with a revolving weathervane to be based on the Giralda, the bell tower that adjoins the cathedral at Seville (see fig. 36). Knowing of Saint-Gaudens's interest in modeling a sculpture of a female nude, White asked him to produce the tower's finial. Saint-Gaudens took on the project as a labor of love, asking only for compensation for his expenses. He based the facial features of *Diana*, the only female nude in his oeuvre, on an under lifesize bust portrait of Davida Johnson Clark (1861–1910) from 1886 (fig. 37). The Swedish-born Clark (fig. 38) had been his model, mistress, and muse since the early 1880s, and in 1889 she became the mother of his second son, Louis P. Clark.

In November 1891 the first version of *Diana* (fig. 39) was hoisted to the top of the tower, 347 feet above the Manhattan streetscape. Composed of hammered and gilded

Fig. 37 Augustus Saint-Gaudens. *Davida Johnson Clark*, 1886. Plaster, shellac; 10½ x 6½ x 6½ in. (26.7 x 16.5 x 16.5 cm). The Metropolitan Museum of Art, Purchase, Gift of Alice and Evelyn Blight and Mrs. William Payne Thompson, by exchange, 2003 (2003.303) (cat. 24)

Fig. 38 Davida Johnson Clark

sheet copper riveted over a steel armature, the eighteen-foot figure surmounted an orb and twelve-foot crescent moon studded with faceted glass prisms. With her billowing drapery and raised bow and arrow, she was intended to revolve in the wind, but because of her great weight (1,800 pounds), she could not perform the intended function. Furthermore, both Saint-Gaudens and White acknowledged that the figure was disproportionately large for the tower, and in September 1892 it was removed. *Diana* was shipped to Chicago, where it topped the central dome of McKim, Mead & White's Agriculture Building for the 1893 World's Columbian Exposition. (The lower half of the figure burned in 1894; the remainder was destroyed sometime after appearing in the 1909 Saint-Gaudens memorial exhibition at the Art Institute of Chicago.)

Fig. 39 First version of *Diana* (1886–91) at the W. H. Mullins Manufacturing Company, Salem, Ohio

Fig. 40 Second version of *Diana* (1892–93) at the W. H. Mullins Manufacturing Company, Salem, Ohio

At thirteen feet, the second, streamlined version of *Diana* (fig. 40) met with far greater success. Elevated to her aerial perch in November 1893, she remained on top of Madison Square Garden's tower until 1925, when the arena was razed. (In about 1905 the swirling draperies were blown off by heavy winds.) Seven years later the sculpture was given to the Philadelphia Museum of Art (fig. 41). Though the public prominence of the nude figure attracted the inevitable criticism, *Diana* became a much-loved icon and until 1908 was the highest point on the New York City skyline. She and her larger predecessor gleamed in the sunlight and were incandescently lit at night (they were the first American sculptures to be illuminated by electricity).

By 1894 Saint-Gaudens was growing savvy to the potential for additional steady income from his successful monuments. The "age of bronze" had come upon America hand in hand with the Aesthetic Movement mania for the artfully planned interior. A market for collectible bronze statuettes was developing, and Saint-Gaudens was among the first American

Fig. 41 Augustus Saint-Gaudens. *Diana*, 1892–93. Sheet copper, h. 14 ft. 6 in. (4.42 m). Philadelphia Museum of Art, Gift of the New York Life Insurance Company, 1932 (1932-30-1)

Fig. 42 Augustus Saint-Gaudens. *Diana*, 1893–94 (this cast, 1894 or after). Bronze, 28¼ x 16¼ x 14 in. (71.8 x 41.3 x 35.6 cm). The Metropolitan Museum of Art, Gift of Lincoln Kirstein, 1985 (1985.353) (cat. 38)

sculptors to copyright and commercially cast his bronzes in unlimited editions, making small changes from model to model. In January 1895 he copyrighted *Diana* and began casting variant reductions, without the swirling drapery of the originals. The first version, a thirty-one-inch figure on a half-sphere (an example of which is in the Brooklyn Museum), was soon followed by the rarest type, a twenty-one-inch figure on a full orb surmounting a two-tier base (fig. 42). A third variant, modeled in Paris in 1899, is the most decorative: a twenty-one-inch figure on a tall tripod base adorned with griffins, scrollwork, and rosettes (an example is in the National Gallery of Art, Washington, D.C.). In addition to *Diana*, during Saint-Gaudens's lifetime reductions of *The Puritan* (cat. 27), *Amor Caritas* (fig. 50), *Head of Victory* (fig. 63), and circular and rectangular variants of the Robert Louis Stevenson relief (fig. 34, cat. 30) were cast in French and American foundries. The bronzes were then sold from showrooms such as Tiffany & Co. and Gorham in New York and Doll and Richards in Boston. *The Puritan*, in particular, was a perennial favorite.

The 1890s saw Saint-Gaudens assume a new role as elder statesman for American sculptors. In 1889 he was elected an academician at the National Academy of Design, a measure of the mainstream acceptance of his Beaux-Arts aesthetics. The goal of establishing a dedicated group of French-trained American sculptors working on American shores had largely been met, and now a second generation of artists, many of them with connections to Saint-Gaudens through his studio and his teaching, vied for the ample supply of commissions for monumental and decorative architectural sculpture. Saint-Gaudens was a generous mentor, a role he very much enjoyed, and as a result he was frequently consulted on professional matters and issues concerning the development of younger sculptors' careers. He was asked, for instance, to be an art advisor for several major civic building programs, including McKim, Mead & White's Boston Public Library and the Library of Congress in Washington, D.C.

For the World's Columbian Exposition in Chicago in 1893, a delayed quadro-centennial celebration of Christopher Columbus's landing in America, Saint-Gaudens served as sculptural advisor to architect Daniel Burnham, the fair's director of works, as well as a juror for the Department of Fine Arts. To Burnham he excitedly remarked: "Look here, old fellow, do you realize that this is the greatest meeting of artists since the fifteenth century!"[13] He recommended MacMonnies, Daniel Chester French, and other sculptors to receive career-enhancing commissions for the ambitious decoration of the Court of Honor. Saint-Gaudens himself was represented (and then unofficially) only by *Diana* on the Agriculture Building, though he did receive a controversy-fraught commission for the fair's presentation medal (cat. 36). He also supervised his assistant Mary Lawrence on the sculpting of a monumental figure of Columbus for the fair (1892–93; destroyed), giving her full credit for the work.

The collegial spirit that allowed the completion of the ambitious outdoor sculpture program at the Chicago exposition became the impetus for the founding in 1893 of the National Sculpture Society (NSS). Saint-Gaudens, along with other senior sculptors like John Quincy Adams Ward and Daniel Chester French, was an original member of the executive council. The primary goals of the NSS were to foster a democratic taste for sculpture and to ensure fair competitions for monumental commissions. The society, still active today, also instigated a program of exhibitions that allowed sculptors to show their smaller works in optimal conditions, without the distracting primacy of paintings.

Fig. 43 Augustus Saint-Gaudens; architectural setting designed by Charles McKim. Shaw Memorial, Boston Common, Boston, 1884–97. Bronze

Saint-Gaudens was intimately involved as well in the development of the American Academy in Rome, the brainchild of Charles McKim. In 1894 McKim began planning for an atelier-like program for architecture students that was first known as the American School of Architecture. Saint-Gaudens advised on its sculptural counterpart, the Rinehart Scholarship (named for the late sculptor William Rinehart) established in 1895 to fund four years' study in Paris or Rome. Until the assimilation of these two organizations in 1905 into the American Academy in Rome, Saint-Gaudens assisted with fundraising, his greatest coup being his successful "$100,000 letter" to Henry Clay Frick.

Saint-Gaudens's greatest allegiance, however, was to the creative challenges of his monumental work. Above all, he devoted himself to the memorial to Colonel Robert Gould Shaw (1837–1863) and the Fifty-fourth Massachusetts Regiment (fig. 43), located on the edge of Boston Common across from the Massachusetts State House. Plans for the memorial began in 1865 and escalated during the 1870s. Saint-Gaudens started his courtship of sorts of the Shaw Memorial Committee in 1881 at the urging of architect Henry Hobson Richardson (the two first met in 1872 and collaborated on several projects, Saint-Gaudens providing architectural sculpture for Richardson's buildings).

Saint-Gaudens met with committee members in 1882. Two years—and countless studies and plans—later, he officially earned the commission. His first equestrian statue, the monument would occupy him intensely for the next thirteen years.

Colonel Robert Gould Shaw was just twenty-five when he and the troops of the Fifty-fourth Massachusetts Regiment, the first African American volunteer regiment of the Union Army, set off southward from Boston in May 1863. Their day of reckoning came on July 18, during the assault on Fort Wagner in Charleston Harbor. When Shaw and his troops attacked the fort on foot, almost half of them, including Shaw, lost their lives to Confederate artillery fire. The abolitionist Shaw family wanted a monument that would honor the bravery and sacrifice of not only their own son but also the men of the Fifty-fourth. From early pencil and clay sketches of Shaw alone, Saint-Gaudens moved to a conception with the colonel on horseback, with the foot soldiers marching alongside as in syncopated freeze-frame rhythm. For his likeness of Shaw Saint-Gaudens drew on photographs and family input, but for the infantrymen he used live models, some hired off the street. Of the approximately forty distinctly individualized head sketches he made at one-third life size (see fig. 44), sixteen were incorporated into the model. From the young drummer boy at the front to the stoic marchers behind Shaw, these portraits rank among the finest and most sensitive sculptural likenesses of African Americans. Every detail, from the random diagonals of the raised weapons to the folds of the pant legs, is integral to the rightward procession of the troops marching down Beacon Street, off to the uncertain fate of battle.

Starting with the Farragut Monument, Saint-Gaudens employed an affecting—and effective—thematic device in his work that amplified the overall narrative by synthesizing the real and the ideal, the material and the spiritual, harnessing a naturalistic portrait to an allegorical figure. In the Shaw Memorial the figure floating above the troops encompasses and forecasts both the angel of death and the angel of victory. Grasping poppies symbolizing eternal sleep as well as laurel branches for glory, she serves as a poignant reminder that the monument is above all consecrated to national duty and valor.

Saint-Gaudens was a notoriously slow worker who could drive monument committee members to exasperation. He himself admitted that his work "dragged in most cases to lengths which would have taxed the patience of angels."[14] Yet even for him the thirteen years it took to complete the Shaw Memorial was an extreme case. His drive for compositional and technical perfection resulted in many rounds of sketches, modifications, enlargements, and reworking of details. Finally, in spring 1897, the Shaw model was cast at the Gorham Manufacturing Company in Providence, Rhode Island, one of the leading American bronze foundries of the day. Gorham rose admirably to the technical challenge of casting a sculpture with a complex synthesis of low and high relief and elements in the

Fig. 44 Augustus Saint-Gaudens. *Sketch Model of Soldier's Head for the Shaw Memorial*, 1883–93 (this cast, late 1940s). Bronze, 5¾ x 3¾ x 5½ in. (14.6 x 9.5 x 14 cm). United States Department of the Interior, National Park Service, Saint-Gaudens National Historic Site, Cornish, New Hampshire, Gift to the Saint-Gaudens Memorial by John O'Connor Jr.

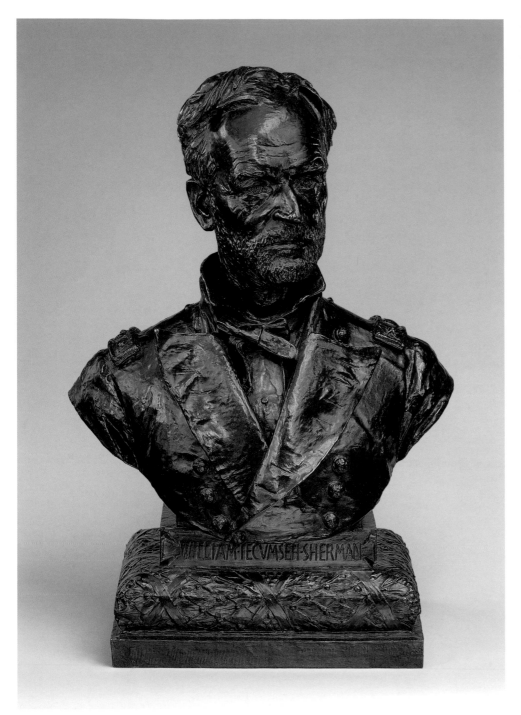

Fig. 45 Augustus Saint-Gaudens. *General William Tecumseh Sherman*, 1888 (this cast, 1910). Bronze, 31¼ x 21½ x 12½ in. (79.4 x 54.6 x 31.8 cm). The Metropolitan Museum of Art, Gift by subscription through the Saint-Gaudens Memorial Committee, 1912 (12.76.2) (cat. 32)

round. The bronze is encased in a classicizing surround of Charles McKim's design, a stone framework with Ionic pilasters topped by a curved cornice and centered between two English elms. Within the rectangular terrace overlooking the Boston Common, a street-level viewing area with benches on the ends was created.

The Shaw Memorial was unveiled on May 31, 1897. The ceremony included a parade led by sixty-five veterans of the Fifty-fourth Regiment and orations by Booker T. Washington and others. Of all of Saint-Gaudens's monuments, this one has attracted the most ongoing scholarly and popular notice. (It served, for instance, as an inspiration for the 1989 film *Glory*.) Generally heralded as Saint-Gaudens's supreme achievement, it is a "living monument" to the contributions of African Americans to the Union cause (during a major restoration that began in 1981 the names of men in the Fifty-fourth who were killed in action were carved onto the back face of the stone setting). Its continuing relevance is proof of his credo that "a sculptor's work endures for so long that it is next to a crime for him to neglect to do everything that lies in his power to execute a result that will not be a disgrace. . . . It is plastered up before the world to stick and stick for centuries, while men and nations pass away."[15]

His American career was riding high when in October 1897 Saint-Gaudens uprooted himself from New York and relocated to Paris. He had been finding it increasingly difficult to work in the city; in order to dodge a constant flow of visitors to his main studio on Thirty-sixth Street he was forced to take on other spaces so that he could sculpt productively. He longed to devote himself intensively to modeling a monument to General William Tecumseh Sherman (1820–1891) for which he had received a commission in 1892 and which he had promised to finish by 1894. And he also felt that it was time to test himself in the company of the world's leading sculptural talent, to become an artist not just of national but also of international repute.

Saint-Gaudens set up his studio at 3 *bis*, Rue de Bagneux, on the Left Bank, and filled it with studio paraphernalia and plaster models that had been shipped from the U.S. He renewed contacts with old colleagues such as John Singer Sargent. He befriended James A. M. Whistler, who was a frequent visitor at the studio, and Auguste Rodin, whose studio he called at in 1899 to see *The Gates of Hell*. Saint-Gaudens traveled often, including to London to see Edward Burne-Jones's memorial exhibition, to the Pyrenees to visit his father's birthplace, and to Amiens to admire the cathedral with Henry Adams. He also completed several commissioned portrait busts and reliefs, including, in 1899, a low-relief marble of Colonel Shaw's older sister Josephine (cat. 43).

But, as he had intended, Saint-Gaudens occupied himself principally with the Sherman Monument. The venerated Civil War hero was celebrated for his triumphant "March to the Sea" in 1864, when he moved his troops three hundred miles through Georgia to Savannah in twenty-four days. The contract with the Sherman Monument Committee called for Saint-Gaudens to model an equestrian statue with a figure of Victory installed on an architect-designed pedestal "with all its appurtenances finished and complete."[16] The basis for the monument was a vigorously naturalistic portrait bust that Saint-Gaudens had modeled from life in 1888 (fig. 45), capturing the general's independent and feisty spirit in such details as the hawkish glare, stubbly face, and askew cravat. The sculptor had also been summoned by Sherman's family upon his death in 1891 to take a death mask. While he was still in New York Saint-Gaudens had called upon his occasional assistant Alexander Phimister Proctor to create the horse for the monument. Proctor and Saint-Gaudens selected as a model a famous jumper named Ontario, who was boarded in a Central Park riding academy and was brought to the sculptor's Fifty-ninth Street studio by his handler. Proctor completed the horse in 1895, a full two years before Saint-Gaudens went abroad to finish the sculpture.

Once in Paris Saint-Gaudens worked obsessively on the winged allegorical figure of Victory that he had begun modeling in New York in early 1897. First, as was his custom, he sculpted the figure undraped. He used a highly sought-after artists' model, Hettie Anderson (see fig. 46), an African American woman whom he said had "a figure like a goddess."[17] Later, in Paris, he found the arrangement of the drapery for the clothed version of Victory particularly challenging, spending two weeks arranging flowing cloth

Fig. 46 Anders Zorn (1860–1920). *Augustus Saint-Gaudens and His Model*, 1897. Etching with retroussage, single state; plate 5⅜ x 7¾ in. (13.7 x 19.8 cm), sheet 9⅞ x 12¾ in. (25.2 x 32.4 cm). The Metropolitan Museum of Art, Harris Brisbane Dick Fund, 1917 (17.3.726) (cat. 52)

on four different models to arrive at the desired swirling, windswept effect. *Victory* (fig. 47), in her classicizing chiton, wears a crown of laurel on her head and holds a palm branch in her left hand. In the final monument (see fig. 53), Victory leads Sherman to battle and ultimately to peace; together they surge forward—cape, gown, and horse's tail billowing dramatically.

Long-awaited honors and appreciative critical recognition were lavished on Saint-Gaudens in his showings at the Paris Salons of 1898 and 1899 and, especially, the Exposition Universelle of 1900. Displayed to great acclaim in 1899 were a full-size model of the horse and rider for the Sherman Monument and a reduced model of the group that included the figure Victory. The result elicited a rapturous letter from Saint-Gaudens to his son: "I have got a swelled head for the first time in my life for the Sherman really looks bully and is smashingly fine. . . . Occasionally I fall on my knees and adore it."[18]

At the same moment, the French government ordered a bronze cast of Saint-Gaudens's *Amor Caritas* for the Musée du Luxembourg (now in the collection of the Musée d'Orsay). The winged *Amor Caritas*, like the Shaw Memorial, underwent years of revisions as Saint-Gaudens pursued perfection. The ethereal figure, Pre-Raphaelite in ethos, with its solemn facial expression, frontal pose, and free-flowing draperies, first appeared in 1879 as one of three oversize angels on the Edwin D. Morgan family tomb at Cedar Hill Cemetery in Hartford, Connecticut (see fig. 48; the incomplete marble carvings were destroyed by fire in 1884). She reappeared, each time with modifications, in the form of the marble caryatids Amor and Pax Saint-Gaudens sculpted for the Vanderbilt house in 1881–83 (see fig. 16); in his marble memorial to Ann Maria Smith of 1887 in Island Cemetery, Newport, Rhode Island; and in the John Judson Hall tomb of 1891 in Sleepy Hollow Cemetery, Tarrytown, New York (see fig. 49). Their high-relief successor, *Amor Caritas* (fig. 50), was completed in 1898, the beauty now wearing a crown and a belt of passionflowers and bearing an upraised ornamental tablet inscribed AMOR CARITAS (Love, Charity). *Amor Caritas* was later translated to marble for the Maria Mitchell Memorial (1902) in Saint Stephen's Church in Philadelphia

Fig. 47 Augustus Saint-Gaudens. *Victory*, 1892–1903 (this cast, 1914 or after, by 1916). Bronze, gilt; 38 x 9½ x 18½ in. (96.5 x 24.1 x 47 cm).
The Metropolitan Museum of Art, Rogers Fund, 1917 (17.90.1) (cat. 44)

Fig. 48 Mariana Griswold Van Rensselaer, *Book of American Figure Painters* (Philadelphia: J. B. Lippincott Company, 1886). Title page, with a reproduction of the central angel for the Edwin D. Morgan family tomb at Cedar Hill Cemetery, Hartford, Connecticut

Fig. 49 Augustus Saint-Gaudens in his Paris studio, 1898, with a plaster model for the John Judson Hall tomb at Sleepy Hollow Cemetery in Sleepy Hollow, New York

(since 2005 in the Philadelphia Museum of Art). In this series Saint-Gaudens's creative process, refinement of detail, and ideal of female beauty gradually unfold before us in three dimensions.

The Paris Exposition Universelle, open to the public between April and November 1900, attracted some fifty million visitors. In addition to serving on the American committee for the sculpture installation, Saint-Gaudens was represented by four major monuments, as well as a group of fourteen low-relief portrait medallions (which he donated to the Musée du Luxembourg at the same time *Amor Caritas* was purchased). The completed plaster model for the Sherman Monument was displayed in the central glass-roofed area of the Grand Palais, the focal point among a half-circle grouping of sculptures allocated to the Americans (fig. 51). At the top of a sweeping staircase to the second floor stood a plaster model of the Shaw Memorial, the fourth and final version that Saint-Gaudens had continued to rework (notably in the positioning of the floating angel and the disposition of her draperies) even after the dedication of the bronze (fig. 43) in 1897 (the plaster model is now on loan to the National Gallery of Art, Washington, D.C., by the Saint-Gaudens National Historic Site). Also on view were plaster casts of *Amor Caritas* and *The Puritan*, the latter on the fairgrounds outdoors. For his

Fig. 50 Augustus Saint-Gaudens. *Amor Caritas*, 1880–98 (this cast, 1918). Bronze, gilt; 103¼ x 50 in. (262.3 x 127 cm). The Metropolitan Museum of Art, Rogers Fund, 1918 (19.124) (cat. 42)

Fig. 51 Plaster model for the Sherman Monument in the installation at the Exposition Universelle, Paris, 1900

Fig. 52 Saint-Gaudens and his assistants James Earle Fraser, Henry Hering, Elsie Ward, and others in his Cornish studio with the plaster model for the Sherman Monument, 1901

participation in the exposition Saint-Gaudens was awarded the top honor, the Grand Prix, as was his one-time studio assistant MacMonnies.

Fig. 53 Augustus Saint-Gaudens; base designed by Charles McKim. Sherman Monument, Grand Army Plaza, New York, 1892–1903. Gilded bronze

"This Paris experience," Saint-Gaudens said in 1899, "as far as my art goes, has been a great thing for me. . . . I see my place clearly now; I know, or think I know, just where I stand. A great self-confidence has come over me, and a tremendous desire and will to achieve high things."[19] Now welcomed as an artist of global stature, he was named a correspondent of both the Institut de France and the Société Nationale des Beaux-Arts, and in 1901 he was awarded the prestigious Chevalier de la Legion d'Honneur. In 1906 the Royal Academy of Arts in London named him an honorary foreign academician. This shower of accolades abroad ("Wings are beginning to sprout on my shoulders," he wrote)[20] was matched in the United States with honorary degrees from Princeton (1897), Harvard (1897), and Yale (1905). Saint-Gaudens was elected to the National Academy of Arts and Letters (now the American Academy of Arts and Letters) in 1904, the same year as writers William D. Howells and Samuel Clemens.

Saint-Gaudens's triumphs during his Paris sojourn were overshadowed, however, by medical issues. He had for years suffered from bouts of depression (in those days diagnosed as neurasthenia) that at times left him with "a complete absence of ambition."[21]

45

Soon after the opening of the Exposition Universelle he was diagnosed with an intestinal tumor, and in July 1900 he returned to Boston for surgery at Massachusetts General Hospital. Settling year-round in Cornish, he spent his final years in periods of greater and lesser comfort, treating his cancer not only with the conventional medicine of the day but also through experimental diets (no breakfast, for instance, and six small meals a day) and electric current treatments. He also enjoyed Cornish's recreational offerings (and imposed mandatory leisure time on his posse of some fifteen studio assistants), in winter sporting his trademark muskrat fur hat. His property featured a swimming hole, a nine-hole golf course, and a large toboggan run, and nearby Blow-Me-Down Pond was cleared for skating and hockey. Sleigh and carriage rides were popular pastimes as well.

Despite his illness, Saint-Gaudens continued to work on sculpture commissions, foremost among them the Sherman Monument (see fig. 52). In Cornish he refined compositional details, to the extent that he was making modifications on a duplicate cast of the plaster model while preparations for the bronze casting took place in Paris. He sent changes overseas at first by letter to his trusted molder Gaëtan Ardisson and later by shipping various plaster pieces to be substituted on the model at the foundry. After it was cast at Thiébaut Frères in Paris, the monument was shipped first to the Metropolitan Museum in New York, where it remained only briefly, and then on to Cornish, where it was set up in a field and gilded so that the sculptor could study the effects of light and weather on its surface.

In New York the placement of the Sherman Monument was hotly debated: proposals ranged from the south end of the Mall in Central Park to in front of Ulysses S. Grant's tomb on Riverside Drive. Ultimately space was allocated in Grand Army Plaza at Fifth Avenue and Fifty-ninth Street, and in spring 1903 the heroic gilt-bronze equestrian was set upon a polished pink Bedford granite pedestal of McKim's design (fig. 53). The surface of the base itself is smoothly classicizing, with bronze wreaths inset into the long sides and a dedicatory inscription on the front. In contrast, the top of the pedestal simulates rugged terrain. The bronze hooves of the horse are anchored directly into the stone, as are scattered bronze pine branches that insinuate the Georgian land through which Sherman led his troops. The Sherman Monument was unveiled with great ceremony on Memorial Day, May 30, 1903, to rave reviews. In 1913 it was relocated sixteen feet south of its original site.

Although the Sherman was unquestionably Saint-Gaudens's last great monument, it was not his last. Although he did pass some commissions along to his assistants and close colleagues, until the very end of his life he took on new orders for monuments. Some of these hearkened back to his earlier sculptures and involved alterations to the original compositions. An enlarged rectangular variant (the cigarette now a quill pen and the bed a chaise longue) of *Robert Louis Stevenson* (fig. 34) was installed as a memorial to the author in Saint Giles' Cathedral, Edinburgh, in June 1904. And a variant of *The Puritan* (fig. 26) was cast for the New England Society of Pennsylvania. *The Pilgrim* (1903–4), as it is titled, is easily distinguished from the original by the reverse orientation of the book spine that clearly reads HOLY BIBLE. Unveiled at Philadelphia's City Hall Plaza in 1904, it was moved to nearby Fairmount Park in 1920.

Other projects were for new monuments, none of which were unveiled before Saint-Gaudens's death: one to Phillips Brooks, the longtime rector of Boston's Trinity Church

(1896–1907); one to Charles S. Parnell, Home Rule advocate for the Irish state, in Dublin (1903–7); and a seated statue of Abraham Lincoln for Chicago's Grant Park (1897–1906). Saint-Gaudens allocated the majority of the manual work—modeling, enlarging, and plaster casting—to his most trusted assistants, a new generation of talent that included Henry Hering, James Earle Fraser, and Frances Grimes. Saint-Gaudens himself remained the creative impulse, drawing sketches, offering criticism, and, when he was well enough, working in the studio. Nevertheless, many of the late sculptures that were carried out principally by assistants, particularly the bas-reliefs, lack the master's spark of genius.

Saint-Gaudens also continued in his role of sculptural advisor for major civic projects. He was engaged to advise on the McMillan Plan, named for Senator James McMillan of Michigan, chairman of the Senate Committee on the District of Columbia. Members of the Senate Park Commission formed in 1901—Saint-Gaudens, McKim, Daniel Burnham, and Frederick Law Olmsted—were charged with establishing the architectural master plan for Washington, D.C. The McMillan Plan created the National Mall, which extended from the Capitol Building, past the Washington Monument, to what would eventually be Henry Bacon's Lincoln Monument with Daniel Chester French's *Seated Lincoln* (1911–22). It also called for the building of a new Union Station, an expansive Beaux-Arts structure with a sculpture program by Louis St. Gaudens (completed 1906–13). Following the recommendations of the commission, in 1904 President Theodore Roosevelt established a Board of Public Buildings, more familiarly known as the "Art Cabinet," on which Saint-Gaudens served.

Saint-Gaudens's greatest works, whether large monuments or small bas-reliefs, are tangible reflections of his passion for the creative process and his interest in his subjects. Such was the case with his work for Theodore Roosevelt, from his appointment to the president's Art Cabinet to fulfilling his request that Saint-Gaudens design his special inaugural medal, which was issued in 1905 (fig. 54). In early 1905 Roosevelt, underwhelmed by the mediocrity of American coinage, directed Saint-Gaudens to redesign it to standards matching those of the ancient Greeks. Beginning in 1889 Saint-Gaudens completed several official medallic commissions, but this one was by far the most important. With modeling assistance from Henry Hering, Saint-Gaudens redesigned

Fig. 54 Augustus Saint-Gaudens and Adolph Alexander Weinman (1870–1952). Theodore Roosevelt Special Inaugural Medal (obverse and reverse), 1905. Bronze, diam. 2⅞ in. (7.4 cm). The Metropolitan Museum of Art, Morris K. Jesup Fund, 2008 (2008.112) (cat. 46)

Fig. 55 Augustus Saint-Gaudens. United States ten-dollar gold piece (obverse and reverse), 1907. Diam. 1⅛ in. (2.7 cm). Courtesy of the American Numismatic Society

Fig. 56 Augustus Saint-Gaudens. United States twenty-dollar gold piece (obverse and reverse), 1907. Diam. 1⅜ in. (3.4 cm). Courtesy of the American Numismatic Society

the one-cent, ten-dollar, and twenty-dollar pieces. The one-cent coin (1905–6) for which Saint-Gaudens prepared models was never minted. The ten- and twenty-dollar gold coins—the "eagle" with the head of Liberty in a Native American headdress on the front face and a standing eagle on the reverse and the "double eagle" with a frontal view of Liberty (adapted from the striding Victory on the Sherman Monument) on the obverse and a flying eagle on the reverse—were minted in the fall of 1907, shortly after Saint-Gaudens died. Roosevelt was delighted with what were arguably the most beautiful American coins ever made. The early strikes (figs. 55, 56) are exquisite, but their distinctive high rims, so high that they could not be properly stacked for circulation, necessitated immediate modifications to the dies by Mint engraver Charles E. Barber before the coins' commercial issue (see cats. 48, 49).

In October 1904, while Saint-Gaudens was in New York, he suffered a devastating blow when fire destroyed his Cornish studio and many of the clay sketches and plaster models inside. Studio assistants salvaged what little they could (for instance, a bronze head of the Adams figure), but gone were precious personal papers, drawings and sketches for commissions, and treasured gifts of artwork from John Singer Sargent, Jules Bastien-Lepage, Kenyon Cox, William Merritt Chase, and others. Saint-Gaudens built two new studios, the Studio of the Caryatids, which was destroyed by fire in 1944, and the Little Studio (figs. 57, 58), which stands today on the grounds of the Saint-Gaudens National Historic Site.

Fig. 57 The Little Studio and Aspet, Cornish, New Hampshire, 1990

In 1905 the multitalented Cornish community collaborated to produce "A Masque of 'Ours': The Gods and the Golden Bowl" in honor of Saint-Gaudens's twenty years in Cornish. The masque was written by playwright Louis Shipman and the musical accompaniment by composer Arthur Whiting. The play was performed on a June evening in the field below Aspet on a columned temple stage (fig. 59; in 1914 the temple was replicated in marble and now is the site of Saint-Gaudens's grave). Participants included Kenyon Cox in the role of Pluto and Maxfield Parrish as the centaur Chiron. Touched by this show of

Fig. 58 Saint-Gaudens on the pergola of the Little Studio, Cornish, New Hampshire, 1906

Fig. 59 Performance of "A Masque of 'Ours': The Gods and the Golden Bowl," June 22, 1905, in honor of Saint-Gaudens's twenty years in Cornish, New Hampshire

affection, Saint-Gaudens commemorated the evening with plaquettes decorated with the masque's sylvan setting and inscribed with the names of all the participants. He presented a splendid large gilded version (now in a private collection) to Shipman and in summer 1906 distributed to others small silvered bronzes that had been struck in Paris (fig. 60).

Saint-Gaudens died in Cornish on August 3, 1907, after a seven-year struggle with cancer. Lengthy obituaries in national and international newspapers and journals labeled him the greatest American sculptor and saluted his artistic genius. A simple funeral held in his Cornish studio on August 7 was attended by family, close friends, and assistants past and present. In the months that followed, other gatherings in remembrance of "the Saint" were held in New York, and two monographs and numerous encomiums were published. Several assistants remained at the Cornish studio to finish eight monumental commissions that were near completion. Saint-Gaudens's widow, Augusta, managed the sculptor's estate with shrewdness, always mindful of protecting his memory and his high standards of excellence. While she continued casting good-quality replicas of his small works, her greatest contribution to her husband's legacy was the strategic sale of estate casts to American museums, including the Metropolitan, and, in 1919, the founding of the Saint-Gaudens Memorial in Cornish, a permanent tribute in the form of the studios, home, and sculptures of Saint-Gaudens that are today administered as the Saint-Gaudens National Historic Site by the National Park Service.

Saint-Gaudens epitomized the cosmopolitan American artist at the end of the nineteenth century. His career paralleled decades of tremendous societal transformation, characterized by globalization, industrialization, and immigration. From an immigrant Gaelic-Gallic background Saint-Gaudens rose to success seemingly like a character in a contemporary Horatio Alger dime novel. The lasting imprint of his path survives today not only in his stirring and substantial body of work but also in the success of his efforts to make art accessible, necessary, and real to every one of us.

Fig. 60 Augustus Saint-Gaudens. *Cornish Celebration Presentation Plaquette*, 1905–6. Bronze and silver, 3¼ x 1¾ in. (8.3 x 4.5 cm). The Metropolitan Museum of Art, Gift of Kenyon Cox, 1908 (08.216) (cat. 47)

49

On the evening of March 2, 1908, some two thousand people braved the aftereffects of a day of heavy rain and made their way to The Metropolitan Museum of Art. Attired in evening dress, they alighted from their carriages at the Central Park entrance and presented engraved Tiffany & Co. invitations (fig. 61) for the opening reception of the "Memorial Exhibition of the Works of Augustus Saint-Gaudens." When they arrived in the Hall of Sculpture—what we now know as the Great Hall—visitors passed through a receiving line with Museum director Sir Caspar Purdon Clarke, trustee Joseph Choate, New York City mayor George McClellan, and sculptor Daniel Chester French, who was chairman of the Saint-Gaudens Memorial Committee. As guests wandered through the vast space, they were treated to the music of a twenty-two-piece orchestra, a visual feast of potted plants and bay trees, and most of all, a comprehensive installation of 154 works of art.

This tribute to Saint-Gaudens was one of the most ambitious exhibitions at the Metropolitan to date. It served as testament not only to the sculptor's considerable artistic talents but also to the central role he played as an ambassador of American art at the turn of the twentieth century. His influence, as well as the appeal of his art at the Metropolitan, has been lasting: the memorial exhibition was the first of four solo exhibitions dedicated to Saint-Gaudens held here; two others followed in 1973 and 1985–86, and the fourth opens on June 30, 2009. The Metropolitan now owns some forty-five marbles, bronzes, plasters, and works in other media by Saint-Gaudens, from his early shell cameos to his latest gold coins, from his sketchy bas-relief portraits to his full-size allegorical female figures and character-penetrating portrait busts and statuettes derived from his public monuments. Collectively these varied pieces document the career of an artist who almost single-handedly redirected the course of American sculpture in the late nineteenth century. They also, through their collective provenance, reflect Saint-Gaudens's web of esteemed contacts—artists, writers, financiers, politicians, and other notables of the day who shaped America's international coming of age in art and literature, diplomacy and economics, and social policy and technology.

Like several other leading American artists, Saint-Gaudens worked to foster the Metropolitan's prominent position in the cultural fabric of New York. His first documented interaction with the Museum occurred in 1882, twelve years after its founding, when it had just been installed in the building on the edge of Central Park that it occupies today. To supplement the growing collections, many collectors and artists had lent paintings and sculptures to the new museum, and Saint-Gaudens contributed a plaster low-relief portrait of Sarah Redwood Lee he had completed in 1881 (an example is at Chesterwood, Daniel Chester French's home in Stockbridge, Massachusetts). The Metropolitan was also occasionally a venue for contemporary art displays, including the

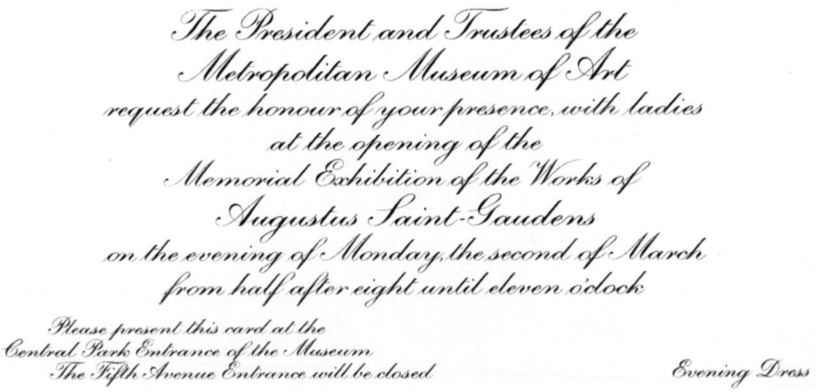

Fig. 61 Tiffany & Co. invitation to the opening of "Memorial Exhibition of the Works of Augustus Saint-Gaudens," 1908

The President and Trustees of the
Metropolitan Museum of Art
request the honour of your presence, with ladies
at the opening of the
Memorial Exhibition of the Works of
Augustus Saint-Gaudens
on the evening of Monday, the second of March
from half after eight until eleven o'clock

Please present this card at the
Central Park Entrance of the Museum
The Fifth Avenue Entrance will be closed                    Evening Dress

Society of American Artists annual exhibition in 1886. Saint-Gaudens, who had helped found that progressive organization in 1877, contributed an ivory-tinted plaster version of *The Children of Jacob H. Schiff* (see fig. 20). This showpiece, installed in the center of one of the second-floor paintings galleries, earned universal critical praise for its decorative treatment of form.

As Saint-Gaudens's career advanced during the 1880s he took on roles as teacher, mentor, and advisor with a sense of duty to his profession and to the advancement of the arts in America. In 1891 Museum president Henry G. Marquand named Saint-Gaudens a Fellow for Life of the Museum and elected him to the Special Committee on Casts (other distinguished committee members included Louis Comfort Tiffany and Stanford White). In addition to raising funds, this committee recommended the purchase of an ample selection of plaster copies after antique and Renaissance sculpture for the Metropolitan's collection. Saint-Gaudens assisted by financing the purchase of a plaster cast after Peter Vischer's bronze statue *King Arthur* in Innsbruck's Hofkirche. He collaborated in a number of acquisitions, among them two American paintings donated to the Museum by "several gentlemen" in 1892–93: *The Rain* (1889) by William Anderson Coffin and *Eleanor Hardy Bunker* (1890) by the recently deceased Dennis Miller Bunker. And in 1898 Saint-Gaudens served on a special committee of the National Sculpture Society to cast eleven bronzes by their departed colleague Olin Levi Warner (1844–1896) for presentation to the Metropolitan.

Saint-Gaudens's interest in the Museum's collections extended to using objects from it as reference points for his own projects. In 1905, for example, a plaster cast after Jean-Antoine Houdon's marble bust *Benjamin Franklin* (1778) served as the basis for the profile portrait on the front face of the Benjamin Franklin Commemorative Medal (cat. 50), the commission that he had passed along to his younger brother Louis St. Gaudens. Also in 1905 Saint-Gaudens requested a copy of a panel depicting a seated woman playing a kithara in a Roman fresco excavated from a villa at Boscoreale (40–30 B.C.), near Pompeii, that had been acquired by the Metropolitan. The copy, by painter-muralist Barry Faulkner, hung in the sculptor's Little Studio in Cornish and served as the inspiration for the figures of Love and Art for two monumental sculptural groups he had been working on since 1892 for the entrance to McKim, Mead & White's Boston Public Library (the groups remained unfinished at his death).

Saint-Gaudens enjoyed easy and collegial relations with Museum trustees and staff, which over the years benefited both artist and institution. For instance, in spring 1902, through the efforts of trustee William E. Dodge (who also served as chairman of the Sherman Statue Committee), the Museum temporarily housed the bronze Sherman Monument (fig. 53) after its arrival from Paris because the pedestal and site at Grand Army Plaza were not yet ready. Dodge revealed to director Luigi Palma di Cesnola that the offer of storage was made in part "to secure the friendship and good will of Mr. Saint-Gaudens for the Museum."[22] After residing in a shed on the Museum's grounds for several months, the equestrian monument was removed to Saint-Gaudens's studio in Cornish for assembly and preparation of the gilded surface. Upon its return to New York in early 1903, the sculpture was temporarily erected on Museum grounds so that finishing touches could be made before its final installation at Fifty-ninth Street in May.

In its early years the Museum's policy enjoined buying works by living American artists (indeed, its first purchase of an American sculpture did not occur until 1905).

Fig. 62 Augustus Saint-Gaudens. George Washington Inaugural Centennial Medal (obverse and reverse), 1889. Bronze, diam. 4½ in. (11.4 cm). The Metropolitan Museum of Art, Gift of Henry G. Marquand, 1890 (90.18.1) (cat. 34)

Before the early 1900s, therefore, the collection was formed through gifts and bequests by prominent local patrons, trustees, and artists. The first works by Saint-Gaudens to be acquired by the Metropolitan, two examples of a bronze George Washington Inaugural Centennial Medal (fig. 62), were donated in 1890 by Museum president Henry Gurdon Marquand, who had served as chair of the Committee on Art and Exhibition for the 1889 Washington Centennial in New York. Marquand gave the Museum two medals so that the obverse and reverse faces could be viewed simultaneously.

In the early years of the twentieth century two events dramatically affected the status of American sculpture at the Metropolitan Museum: an unexpected $5 million bequest by Jacob S. Rogers, head of Rogers Locomotive Works in Paterson, New Jersey, in 1901, and the election of sculptor Daniel Chester French as chairman of the Board of Trustees' Committee on Sculpture in 1903. This fortuitous combination of bountiful funds for acquiring works by living artists and the professional expertise of one of the leading public sculptors of the day launched three active decades of collecting and exhibiting bronzes by Saint-Gaudens and other American Beaux-Arts sculptors. French served as de facto curator of sculpture until his death in 1931, forming the nucleus of the most comprehensive collection of American sculpture anywhere. From time to time he solicited Saint-Gaudens's advice on acquisitions, including a 1907 cast of Edward Kemeys's *Panther and Cubs* (ca. 1878) and a group of plasters by Frenchman Paul Dubois that Saint-Gaudens called "among the finest things in modern sculpture."[23]

When he surveyed the Museum's nascent collection, French was astonished to find that it included only the one relatively minor work (the Washington medal) by an artist of such eminent reputation as Saint-Gaudens. In 1904 Frank Edwin Elwell, curator of sculpture from 1903 to 1905 and a sculptor himself, encouraged Saint-Gaudens to donate a cast of *Robert Louis Stevenson* (fig. 34), but the sculptor thought it unprincipled to give the Museum his own work (rather than sell it at a nominal price).

Further, he confessed to French: "I shrink from having another copy of it stuck up in public. . . . Let us leave Stevenson in peace and I'll try and think of something else to stick up here."[24] He also strongly opposed the acquisition of the bronze relief panel *Apollo* (1881–83; present location unknown) related to his commission for the Cornelius Vanderbilt II mansion, which artist John La Farge offered to sell the Museum in 1906. French demurred to Saint-Gaudens's claim that the *Apollo* panel was not worthy of the Museum and instead bought from him the exquisite bronze *Head of Victory* (fig. 63) derived from a study for the winged figure in the Sherman Monument (fig. 53).

In 1905 New York financier Jacob H. Schiff funded the acquisition for the Metropolitan's collection of marble versions of three reliefs that Saint-Gaudens himself thought would best represent his work. The three portraits—of his own son Homer, of Schiff's children, and of the children of Prescott Hall Butler (figs. 18, 20, 64)—had all been modeled and cast in bronze in the early 1880s. Saint-Gaudens, who was gravely ill with intestinal cancer, was not able to live up to his promise that he would "supervise and finish [the reliefs] for the Museum, with his own hands . . . under the most generous and favorable conditions."[25] The commission was carried out by the foremost carving firm in New York, the Piccirilli Brothers, with finishing touches added by Saint-Gaudens's longtime assistant Frances Grimes. Fortunately, in early 1907 the sculptor was well enough to advise on the appearance of the Museum's cast of *Head of Victory*. French, who managed the casting process on

Fig. 63 Augustus Saint-Gaudens. *Head of Victory*, 1897–1903 (this cast, 1907). Bronze, 8 x 7 x 6½ in. (20.3 x 17.8 x 16.5 cm). The Metropolitan Museum of Art, Rogers Fund, 1907 (07.90) (cat. 45)

Fig. 64 Augustus Saint-Gaudens. *The Children of Prescott Hall Butler*, 1880–81 (this carving, 1906–7). Marble, 24½ x 36 in. (62.2 x 91.4 cm). The Metropolitan Museum of Art, Gift of Jacob H. Schiff, 1905 (05.15.1) (cat. 16)

Saint-Gaudens's behalf, informed the Gorham Manufacturing Company that Saint-Gaudens desired "to pay special attention to the *patine*."[26]

Soon after Saint-Gaudens's death in August 1907 French initiated plans for a memorial exhibition of the sculptor's work, to be held at the Metropolitan with the cooperation of the sculptor's widow, Augusta, and his son Homer. The so-called Saint-Gaudens Memorial Committee, a distinguished group of Saint-Gaudens's friends and fellow cultural figures, was assembled in late October. Among its members were architect Cass Gilbert, painters John La Farge and Kenyon Cox, and sculptors John Quincy Adams Ward and Louis St. Gaudens. The committee of twenty-four, with ex officio members representing the Museum, worked hastily to raise funds, negotiate loans with private lenders, and assemble a catalogue in time for the March 2, 1908, opening. The commemorative exhibition was held in the Great Hall (figs. 65, 66), which since its completion in 1902 had served as the principal gallery for the exhibition of modern European and American sculpture. Ironically, Saint-Gaudens had once likened Richard Morris Hunt's grand space to the Baths of Caracalla in Rome and candidly declared it a dismal space for displaying works of art.

Regardless of Saint-Gaudens's sentiments, the Great Hall had recently been renovated to improve its lighting, so it was empty of the Museum's own sculptures for the Saint-Gaudens exhibition. A runaway success, the show initiated a program of regular special exhibitions at the Museum as well as a series of memorial exhibitions for such distinguished American artists as Thomas Eakins and William Merritt Chase (in 1917) and John Singer Sargent (in 1926). The Saint-Gaudens catalogue sold out after just two weeks and was reissued in a revised and enlarged second edition. Museum hours were extended to include Wednesday evenings, and March attendance exceeded a record 100,000. The closing date was twice extended, and after the exhibition concluded on May 31, 1908, it traveled, in reduced form, to four additional American venues through 1910. Newspapers and journals uniformly commended the Metropolitan's exhibition and lionized Saint-Gaudens: "Great Exhibition Honors Saint-Gaudens," "In Memory of America's Greatest Artist," "A Deserved Tribute to a Great Artist."

In addition to many representative small-scale bronzes, marbles, and plasters, the Saint-Gaudens Memorial Committee had secured for the exhibition full-size plaster casts of several monuments, among them the Farragut Monument, *Abraham Lincoln: The Man (Standing Lincoln)*, the Adams Memorial, and the equestrian Sherman Monument (see figs. 14, 24, 35, 53), this last shipped from Paris in ten crates and reassembled at the south end of the Great Hall. The show also featured the recently cast heroic-size bronze *Abraham Lincoln (Seated Lincoln)* of 1897–1906, destined for Grant Park in Chicago, and Kenyon Cox's grand portrayal of Saint-Gaudens in his Thirty-sixth Street studio (fig. 67). The original painting of 1887 had burned in a disastrous fire in the sculptor's Cornish studio in 1904. At French's request, Cox painted a replica especially for the memorial exhibition, and it was immediately purchased for the Metropolitan Museum through a subscription effort. A number of sculptures lent to the exhibition by their original owners have subsequently entered the Museum's collection. The striking early marble portrait bust of William Maxwell Evarts (fig. 7) was acquired in 1987 and the bronze bas-relief profile of young Rodman de Kay Gilder (cat. 12) in 1994.

Fig. 65 "Memorial Exhibition of the Works of Augustus Saint-Gaudens," Hall of Sculpture, The Metropolitan Museum of Art, view looking south, 1908

Fig. 66 "Memorial Exhibition of the Works of Augustus Saint-Gaudens," Hall of Sculpture, The Metropolitan Museum of Art, view looking north, 1908

After the exhibition closed at the Metropolitan, French and the Saint-Gaudens Memorial Committee turned their attention to fundraising for the acquisition of posthumous bronze casts for the collection. This process took longer than expected, for Augusta Saint-Gaudens proved a formidable and unpredictable negotiator, even threatening to sue the Museum over the ownership of the portrait of Saint-Gaudens by Ellen Emmet Rand (cat. 56). Finally, in 1912, she conceded to donate a bronze bas-relief portrait of Samuel Gray Ward (fig. 19), a founder of the Museum and its first treasurer.

Fig. 67 Kenyon Cox (1856–1919). *Augustus Saint-Gaudens*, 1887 (this replica, 1908). Oil on canvas, 33½ x 47⅛ in. (85.1 x 119.7 cm). The Metropolitan Museum of Art, Gift of friends of the artist, through August F. Jaccaci, 1908 (08.130) (cat. 51)

She also authorized four bronzes to be cast for the Museum from original plasters. (Many of the American bronzes that the Metropolitan acquired during these years were cast on special order, with the result that artists and founders often lavished extra attention on their finishing.)

In 1912 the Museum accessioned bas-reliefs by Saint-Gaudens of French naturalist painter Jules Bastien-Lepage and Scottish writer Robert Louis Stevenson (figs. 12, 34) as well as the busts of Civil War heroes Admiral David Glasgow Farragut and General William Tecumseh Sherman (cat. 13, fig. 45) that had served as artistic fodder for his most prominent New York monuments (figs. 14, 53). The acquisition of the Sherman bust must have been particularly satisfying to Daniel Chester French, as he considered it "one of the finest things [Saint-Gaudens] ever made."[27] After the Saint-Gaudens Memorial Committee was dissolved in 1912 French continued untiringly to increase the Museum's holdings of Saint-Gaudens's sculptures; during his tenure as trustee a remarkable twenty were acquired through gift and purchase.

All purchases of authorized posthumous casts of Saint-Gaudens's sculptures were controlled by Augusta Saint-Gaudens. A shrewd businesswoman, she devoted

Fig. 68 Augustus Saint-Gaudens. *Louise Adele Gould*, 1904. Marble, 16½ x 17 x 4½ in. (41.9 x 43.2 x 11.4 cm). The Metropolitan Museum of Art, Bequest of Charles W. Gould, 1931 (32.62.1) (cat. 41)

herself to perpetuating her husband's memory and worked with the American foundries, in particular Tiffany Studios and Gorham Manufacturing Company, who cast his work. She strategically marketed Saint-Gaudens's sculptures to American museums, selling groups of bronzes to the Detroit Institute of Arts, the Saint Louis Art Museum, and the Brooklyn Institute of Arts and Sciences (now the Brooklyn Museum). At the same time, she and her son, Homer, with the help of Metropolitan trustees George F. Baker, Robert W. de Forest, and Daniel Chester French, established a museum on the grounds of the sculptor's studio and residence in Cornish. The Saint-Gaudens Memorial, as it was first called, is now operated as the Saint-Gaudens National Historic Site by the National Park Service (with the Saint-Gaudens Memorial functioning as an advisory group of trustees).

Fig. 69 *Diana* (cat. 37) on the Great Hall Balcony, The Metropolitan Museum of Art, 1933

Augusta Saint-Gaudens authorized the casting of statuettes and bas-reliefs that Saint-Gaudens had issued as commercial bronzes, eventually expanding the inventory to some twenty-five models. Recognizing their market appeal and income potential, she issued reductions that were never cast during the artist's lifetime. Such was the case with two statuettes that have assumed signature status in Saint-Gaudens's oeuvre: the *Standing Lincoln* derived from the monument in Chicago (see fig. 24) and the winged *Victory* (fig. 47) from the Sherman Monument. Augusta Saint-Gaudens offered to sell both casts to the Museum in 1914, but no action was immediately taken. Three years later, in 1917, Daniel Chester French purchased the gilded *Victory* statuette out of Gorham's Fifth Avenue showroom.

As French was developing the Museum's American sculpture holdings (then classified under the Department of Decorative Arts), he also was lobbying for the prominent display of "modern" American sculpture in the Museum's galleries. In 1918 an "Exhibition of American Sculpture" opened in three galleries flanking the Central Park entrance at the southwest corner of the Museum. The show, curated by French, was in reality a long-term installation, with temporary loans rotating in and out and new acquisitions added as they entered the collection. *Amor Caritas* (fig. 50) was first displayed in this installation as a plaster version, as was the Adams Memorial (fig. 35). Later, in 1919, Museum trustees allocated money from the Rogers Fund to have *Amor Caritas* cast in bronze and substituted the gilded bronze into the installation. In 1925–26, with the completion of the new Wing K designed by McKim, Mead & White, the exhibition was disbanded and American sculpture was allocated to two new galleries on the south end of the first floor, abutting the Roman Court. Seventeen works by Saint-Gaudens dominated this installation, with the Vanderbilt Mantelpiece (fig. 16) commanding the western wall of the larger room.

One measure of Daniel Chester French's success in acquiring Saint-Gaudens's work for the Museum is the number of gifts that came from original owners and next of kin, a steady stream of beneficence that continued throughout the 1910s and 1920s. Thus the Metropolitan acquired Saint-Gaudens's friendship portraits of artists Charles McKim, Francis Davis Millet, and John Singer Sargent (fig. 11, cats. 10, 14), all modeled during their "jolly days" in Paris between 1877 and 1880. Saint-Gaudens cast intimately scaled portraits like these in extremely limited editions, frequently giving them away as tokens of affection or exchanging them for works of art by the sitters (as was the case with Sargent's medal).

Other gifts came from scions of New York's genteel society who had close personal relationships with Saint-Gaudens. Mariana Griswold Van Rensselaer, who championed the sculptor in her published writings, donated her bas-relief in a superlative carved oak frame designed by Stanford White (fig. 31). Charles Gould, a trustee of the Metropolitan from 1915 to 1930, gave and bequeathed three marble portraits of his adored late wife Louise Adele Gould (fig. 68, cats. 39, 40). Charles Burlingham, a close friend of reformer Josephine Shaw Lowell, purchased the marble bas-relief of Lowell (cat. 43) from her estate and presented it to the Museum. One of the most splendid—and atypical—gifts came from Mrs. Cornelius Vanderbilt II in 1925, when her palatial residence at Fifth Avenue and Fifty-seventh Street was razed. Saint-Gaudens's enormous red Numidian marble mantel, originally sited in the house's grand entrance hall, was disassembled and relocated to the Metropolitan (fig. 16).

French's final major acquisition before his death in 1931 was, appropriately, a monumental bronze by Saint-Gaudens. The second version of *Diana*, his only representation of a female nude, had been installed on Madison Square Garden's tower as a weathervane since 1893. When the building was demolished in 1925 New Yorkers lost a landmark, for the thirteen-foot *Diana* was eventually acquired by the Philadelphia Museum of Art, where it remains prominently installed (fig. 41). French's purchase of a gilded bronze cast after a half-size model (cat. 37) allowed this much-loved icon to retain a New York presence. After 1933, when American sculpture was relocated to the first- and second-floor galleries flanking the Grand Staircase, *Diana* was given special status, isolated on a plinth built into a balcony railing (fig. 69). The sculpture remains a familiar landmark in the American Wing, where it has been installed in the center of the Charles Engelhard Court since 1987.

The Great Depression, the Second World War, changing aesthetics, and other factors spelled a fallow period for the acquisition of works by Saint-Gaudens and other "historic" American sculptors at the Metropolitan. The only piece by Saint-Gaudens that entered the collection for several decades was a commercial-quality statuette of *The Puritan* (cat. 27) that was one of fourteen American bronzes in the 1939 bequest of Jacob Ruppert, beer brewer and owner of the New York Yankees. In 1948, the centenary year of Saint-Gaudens's birth, the artist's sculptures were gathered for a retrospective exhibition at the Century Association to which the Metropolitan lent four pieces.

As was true of many other significant American artists, the commercial and scholarly fortunes of Saint-Gaudens's work declined during the middle decades of the twentieth century, only to be revived in the 1970s. In 1973 American Wing curator Lewis I. Sharp brought the Museum's Saint-Gaudens holdings together for the first time in many years for the exhibition "Augustus Saint-Gaudens: Sculpture in the Metropolitan

Museum of Art," and a variant of the show was installed at the Federal Reserve Bank of New York from December 1973 until May 1974. Ambitious American Wing building plans, spurred by the nation's bicentennial, resulted in the opening of the atrium-like Charles Engelhard Court and permanent galleries for American paintings and sculpture in 1980, giving cohesive visual prominence to the American sculpture collection for the first time in decades. In 1985–86 the Engelhard Court was the site of the comprehensive exhibition "Augustus Saint-Gaudens: Master Sculptor" (see fig. 70), curated by Kathryn Greenthal. Among the fifty-seven works on display were the original bronze Farragut Monument from Madison Square Park and the memorial to Robert Louis Stevenson from Saint Giles' Cathedral in Edinburgh. The 1988 opening of the Henry R. Luce Center for the Study of American Art, with its glass cases for open study-storage, made Saint-Gaudens's works in all scales and media accessible after years of inconsistent installation.

Fig. 70 Exhibition "Augustus Saint-Gaudens: Master Sculptor," Charles Engelhard Court, The Metropolitan Museum of Art, 1985–86

These propitious moments launched the second great chapter in the Metropolitan's acquisition of American sculpture, especially works by Saint-Gaudens. Since 1980 seventeen pieces representing all facets of his oeuvre have been acquired. The earliest years of the artist's career are now well represented with the purchase of delicate shell cameos of John Tuffs and Hannah Rohr Tuffs (fig. 3, cat. 2) and the gift from the Wolf family of *Hiawatha* (fig. 4), Saint-Gaudens's first full-scale marble, modeled and carved in Rome. The exquisite jewel-like statuette *Diana* (fig. 42) was a gift of Lincoln Kirstein, a founder of the New York City Ballet and author of book-length essays on the Shaw and Adams memorials. A shellacked plaster portrait of Saint-Gaudens's model and mistress Davida Clark (fig. 37), given to her by the sculptor, represents a more personal side of his oeuvre. And recent purchases of medals, notably the Theodore Roosevelt Special Inaugural Medal (fig. 54), have added luster to the Metropolitan's holdings of this popular segment of Saint-Gaudens's work.

A number of Saint-Gaudens's sculptures acquired by the Museum over the last several decades were until recently in the hands of the descendants of the original owners. From the family of Stanford White, who frequently collaborated with Saint-Gaudens, came the exquisite marble wedding portrait of Bessie Springs Smith White in its original frame and the caricature medallion of Saint-Gaudens, White, and Charles McKim (fig. 30, cat. 8). Descendants of Saint-Gaudens's talented assistant Mary Lawrence donated the bronze portraits of Bessie White and Robert Louis Stevenson that Saint-Gaudens had given her (cats. 22, 30). Five works now at the Metropolitan were once owned by journalist Richard Watson Gilder, Saint-Gaudens's foremost critical advocate. These include a low-relief portrait of the Gilder family (fig. 13), the first plaster by the artist to enter the collection, and a medallion depicting Frances Folsom Cleveland (cat. 31), a birthday gift from Saint-Gaudens to Gilder in 1902.

With its comprehensive array of Saint-Gaudens's sculptures (understandably excepting certain large public monuments), the Metropolitan Museum is able to recount the history of his career and patronage, the progress of his style and technical experimentation, and the development of public commissions like the Sherman Monument. Recent comprehensive renovations to the American Wing allow for ideal viewing of these sculptures. In the Engelhard Court five works by Saint-Gaudens are installed with other monumental sculpture, stained glass, and architectural elements. In the second-floor paintings and sculpture galleries, scheduled to open in 2011, his sculpture will be installed alongside that of other great artists of America's Gilded Age. The New American Wing provides a fitting showcase for Saint-Gaudens's matchless talent and the role he played in creating a broad and appreciative audience for sculpture.

1. Saint-Gaudens 1913, vol. 1, pp. 38–39.
2. Ibid., p. 104.
3. Ibid., p. 113.
4. Ibid., p. 154; Saint-Gaudens to Evarts, [1876] (copy), Saint-Gaudens Papers, microfilm reel 6, frame 10.
5. Louis St. Gaudens to Annetta Johnson St. Gaudens (his wife), October 23, [1902], Saint-Gaudens Papers, microfilm reel 25, frame 43.
6. Saint-Gaudens to Richard Watson Gilder, December 29, 1879, Richard Watson Gilder Papers, Manuscripts and Archives Division, The New York Public Library, Astor, Lenox and Tilden Foundations.
7. Saint-Gaudens 1913, vol. 1, p. 163.
8. Bion to Saint-Gaudens, October 18, 1881 (original letter), Saint-Gaudens Papers, microfilm reel 15, frame 35; English translation, Saint-Gaudens National Historic Site, Cornish, N.H.
9. French 1918, p. 859.
10. Saint-Gaudens 1913, vol. 1, p. 51.
11. Ibid., p. 312.
12. "Eli Bates' Great Gift: Saint-Gaudens' Colossal Statue of Lincoln," *Chicago Tribune*, October 20, 1887, p. 1.
13. Moore 1929, p. 119.
14. "Reminiscences of an Idiot," Saint-Gaudens Papers, microfilm reel 36, frame 585. Saint-Gaudens began dictating his reminiscences in March 1906; these were later heavily edited for the two-volume *Reminiscences* published in 1913.
15. Saint-Gaudens 1913, vol. 2, pp. 78–79.
16. Contract for Sherman Monument, March 1, 1892, Saint-Gaudens Papers, microfilm reel 36, frame 66.
17. Rose Standish Nichols, ed., "Familiar Letters of Augustus Saint-Gaudens," part 1, *McClure's Magazine* 31 (October 1908), p. 606.
18. Saint-Gaudens to Homer Saint-Gaudens, May 2, 1899, Saint-Gaudens Papers, microfilm reel 22, frame 623.
19. Saint-Gaudens to Rose S. Nichols (his niece), May 10, 1898, quoted in Saint-Gaudens 1913, vol. 2, p. 186.
20. Saint-Gaudens to Louis St. Gaudens, December 1, 1899, Saint-Gaudens Papers, microfilm reel 25, frame 168.
21. Saint-Gaudens to Augusta Saint-Gaudens, [1899], Saint-Gaudens 1913, vol. 2, p. 137.
22. William E. Dodge to General Luigi Palma di Cesnola, January 20, 1902, Saint-Gaudens file (Sa236), Office of the Secretary Correspondence Files, MMA Archives. Cesnola remained suspicious of Saint-Gaudens because the sculptor had publicly opposed Cesnola when the director was involved in protracted controversy with Gaston Feuardent over the authenticity of the Museum's Cesnola collection of antiquities in the early 1880s.
23. Saint-Gaudens to Edward Robinson (director of the Museum), June 25, 1906, Madame Paul Dubois file, Office of the Secretary Correspondence Files, MMA Archives.
24. Saint-Gaudens to Daniel Chester French, December 10, 1904, Saint-Gaudens Papers, microfilm reel 1, frames 413–14.
25. "Augustus Saint-Gaudens—Replicas of His Bas-Reliefs of Children" 1906, p. 26.
26. French to A. A. Buck, Gorham Manufacturing Company, January 15, 1907 (copy), Daniel Chester French Family Papers, Manuscript Division, Library of Congress, Washington, D.C., microfilm reel 1, frame 545.
27. Daniel Chester French to Frederick S. Wait, October 10, 1907, Saint-Gaudens Replica Fund file (Sa237), Office of the Secretary Correspondence Files, MMA Archives.

The quotation in the Author's Acknowledgments on page 80 is from a letter from Henry W. Kent to Robert W. de Forest, March 3, 1908, Saint-Gaudens Loan Exhibition file (L7806), Office of the Secretary Records, MMA Archives.

## Exhibition Checklist

Works in the Collection of The Metropolitan Museum of Art

AUGUSTUS SAINT-GAUDENS (1848–1907)

### 1. John Tuffs                                                    (fig. 3)

ca. 1861
Shell; 1¾ x 1½ in. (4.5 x 3.8 cm), case 2⅝ x 2⅜ x ¾ in. (6.7 x 6 x 1.9 cm)
Purchase, Sheila W. and Richard J. Schwartz Gift and Morris K. Jesup
Fund, 1990 (1990.78.1a, b)

### 2. Hannah Rohr Tuffs

1872
Shell; 2 x 1½ in. (5.1 x 3.8 cm), case 2⅝ x 2⅜ x ¾ in. (6.7 x 6 x 1.9 cm)
Purchase, Sheila W. and Richard J. Schwartz Gift and Morris K. Jesup
Fund, 1990 (1990.78.2a, b)

Shell cameos are created by dexterously cutting away a layer (or layers)
of shell so that the white surface appears superimposed on a background of contrasting color. While he was an apprentice to cameo
cutter Louis Avet, Saint-Gaudens executed this posthumous portrait
of New York attorney John Tuffs (1812–1859), presumably relying on
a daguerreotype that recorded the difficult three-quarter pose. The
delicate wisps of hair, cleft chin, and fashionable cravat reveal Saint-
Gaudens's growing technical confidence, but his rendering of Tuffs's
wandering left eye shows his youthful inexperience.

The likeness must have satisfied Tuffs's widow Hannah Rohr Tuffs
(1829–1905), for in 1872, when visiting Rome with her sister (see cat. 5),
she ordered her own portrait as a companion piece. Saint-Gaudens,
by then a practicing sculptor who cut cameos for additional income,
expertly rendered her features in sharp profile. Her attire reflects a
prim simplicity, but the elaborate hairstyle imparts an elegant touch.
Like many of Saint-Gaudens's cameos, these two are unsigned. They
can be firmly attributed to him through their provenance, however,
for both descended in the Rohr family until their acquisition by the
Metropolitan. They are housed in their original leather-bound cases
with velvet linings.

3

DANIEL HUNTINGTON (1816–1906)

### 3. Anna Watson Stuart

ca. 1862
Oil on canvas, 50 x 40 in. (127 x 101.6 cm)
Gift of Mrs. Denny Brereton, 1943 (43.55.2)

Daniel Huntington, one of Saint-Gaudens's teachers at the National
Academy of Design, was the preferred portraitist of respectable New
York society during the 1860s. Here Mrs. Joseph L. (Anna Watson)
Stuart (1817–1881), wife of an Irish-born dry goods merchant turned
banker, is seated in a lush landscape. She is dressed in fashionable
ermine and laces, and on her right wrist she wears a cameo bracelet
created by Saint-Gaudens. This family heirloom, now in a private
collection, is Saint-Gaudens's most ambitious extant cameo project,
featuring portraits of Joseph (1803–1874) and Anna Stuart and their
four children, Anna (1840–1902), Joseph Jr. (1843–1890), Margaret
(1845–1932), and Robert Watson (1847–1920). Each cameo is set in a
gold mount with a seed pearl border. Saint-Gaudens also completed a
second version of the bracelet (now at the Saint-Gaudens National
Historic Site in Cornish, New Hampshire) without the seed pearls and
the portraits of Joseph Senior and Robert.

The painting was given to the Metropolitan by the granddaughter
of the sitter.

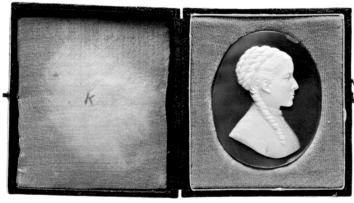

2

## 4. Hiawatha (fig. 4)

1871–72 (this carving, 1874)
Marble, 60 x 34½ x 37¼ in. (152.4 x 87.6 x 94.6 cm)
Gift of Diane, Daniel, and Mathew Wolf, in memory of Catherine
Hoover Voorsanger, 2001 (2001.641)

Since the early 1840s several American sculptors, from expatriates
Hiram Powers and Thomas Crawford to New York–based John
Quincy Adams Ward, have modeled ambitious full-size compositions
of Native American figures. Saint-Gaudens looked to Henry Words-
worth Longfellow's influential epic poem "The Song of Hiawatha"
(1855) for his distinctly American subject. He depicted the Chippewa
chief seated nude on a rock "pondering musing in the forest on the
welfare of his people," as the inscription on the base excerpted from
Longfellow's poem attests. The arrow Hiawatha once held in his right
hand is missing; his quiver and bow are propped against the nearby
ivy-twined tree stump. The ideal subject, minutiae of narrative detail,
and marble medium are telling references to a romanticizing
Neoclassicism that Saint-Gaudens experimented with only briefly.

Saint-Gaudens's first ambitious large-scale sculpture, executed soon
after he arrived in Rome in 1871, attracted two prominent American
patrons: Montgomery Gibbs, who paid to have it cast in plaster from
the clay, and Edwin D. Morgan, who funded its carving in marble and
displayed it in his New York City house (plans to display it in Central
Park were not realized). After Morgan's death in 1883 Hiawatha was
on loan to the Metropolitan from June 1885 until shortly after his
collection was auctioned in January 1886. It was purchased by Judge
Henry Hilton and was for many years installed outdoors on his estate
in Saratoga Springs, New York, hence the weathered appearance of the
marble surface. The sculpture retains its original twenty-three-inch
granite pedestal.

## 5. Eva Rohr (fig. 5)

1872
Marble, 18⅝ x 9¼ x 6½ in. (47.3 x 23.5 x 16.5 cm)
Gift of Allan H. Smith, 1990 (1990.317)

An aspiring opera singer, Eva Rohr (1845–1916) was the youngest
daughter of the twelve children of John Rohr, the successful publisher
of the German-language newspaper the New Yorker Staats-Zeitung.
When he died in 1872 Rohr was said to be one of the five wealthiest
Americans. Early in 1872 Eva and her sister Hannah Rohr Tuffs
visited Rome, where Eva studied opera. Through the bustling American expatriate social circle they encountered Saint-Gaudens. In addition
to introducing him to prospective clients and commissioning her
own cameo (cat. 2), Mrs. Tuffs ordered this marble portrait bust of
her younger sister, the sculptor's first bust commission.

Saint-Gaudens depicted Eva Rohr as the village maid Marguerite
in Charles-François Gounod's opera Faust (after the poem by Goethe),
which had debuted in Paris in 1859. The inscription on the Gothic-
style square base—"I'm neither / Lady neither fair / And home I can /
go without your / care"—refers to the moment at the end of act two
when the virtuous Marguerite rebukes the offer of the besotted philoso-
pher Faust to escort her home. Whether the well-known soprano role
held special significance for Eva is not known.

## 6. William Maxwell Evarts (fig. 7)

1872–73 (this carving, 1874)
Marble, 22⅞ x 12¾ x 9¼ in. (58.1 x 32.4 x 23.5 cm)
Gift of Erving and Joyce Wolf, in memory of Diane R. Wolf, 1987
(1987.405)

Early in his career Saint-Gaudens secured several distinguished
commissions for portrait busts of middle-aged male sitters, all of
which he executed in the hybrid real-ideal style that was customary
at the time. William Maxwell Evarts, by far the finest of the group,
depicts the prominent attorney (1818–1901) as a modern-day Cicero.
The bust is a vigorous naturalistic portrait coupled with an ennobling
herm termination and classicizing undraped chest. In Evarts's hawkish
face, masterfully carved in unsparing detail, marble yields to simulate
flesh. Evarts sat for his portrait in 1872 in the dressing room of his
Second Avenue home. When Saint-Gaudens returned to Rome he
took the plaster model with him and had it translated to marble at
the hands of skilled Italian carvers.

When he first met Saint-Gaudens in Rome, Evarts was based in
Geneva as the United States counsel for the Alabama Claims Tribunal,
which was convened to review sanctions against the British for aiding
the Confederate cause during the Civil War. Later, he served as secretary
of state in Rutherford B. Hayes's administration (1877–81) and as a
United States senator from New York (1885–91). Evarts proved to be
one of Saint-Gaudens's most valuable early contacts, both commissioning copies of marble busts after the antique (see fig. 6) and introducing him to potential American clients in Rome and New York. This
marble bust was included in Saint-Gaudens's memorial exhibition at
the Metropolitan in 1908. It remained in the Evarts family until it
entered the Museum's holdings in 1987.

Designed by James Horton Whitehouse (1833–1922); manufactured by
Tiffany & Co. (founded 1837); at least five of the six medallions on the
body modeled by Augustus Saint-Gaudens; chased by Eugene J.
Soligny (1833–1901)

## 7. The Bryant Vase (fig. 9)

1875–76
Silver; 33½ x 14 x 11¼ in. (85.1 x 35.6 x 28.7 cm), diam. 11¼ in. (28.7 cm);
452 oz. 16 dwt. (14084.2 g)
Gift of William Cullen Bryant, 1877 (77.9a, b)

Like many American artists of his day Saint-Gaudens was versatile,
due both to the necessity of earning income and to the creative
challenges of working in a range of media. In the first decade of his
professional career he painted murals, designed stained glass, and
modeled elements for presentation silver. Shortly after returning to
New York in 1875 he took on work for Tiffany & Co. The most prestigious of his contributions to Tiffany's was modeling medallions for
a vase celebrating the life of poet and New York Evening Post editor
William Cullen Bryant (1794–1878). On the occasion of Bryant's
eightieth birthday on November 3, 1874, his cultural confreres, in the
form of the Bryant Testimonial Commission, announced their intent
to raise funds for a commemorative silver vase. A design competition
was held in February 1875, with James Horton Whitehouse of Tiffany
& Co. producing the winning entry.

Whitehouse's Grecian-form urn on a stepped base is decorated
with eclectic motifs referencing Bryant's poems, interests, and causes,
as well as American flora. At least five of the six Renaissance Revival

medallions around the body of the vase are attributed to Saint-Gaudens. On one side a portrait of the elderly, bearded Bryant is bracketed on the left by Bryant and his father looking at a bust of the poet Homer and on the right by Bryant contemplating a landscape setting. The medallions on the other side depict, from left to right: Bryant as a journalist, allegorical representations of Poetry and Nature, and Bryant as a translator of Homer.

Saint-Gaudens submitted his designs to Tiffany's for production by early 1876, when he received payment. The actual chasing of the repoussé reliefs was carried out by Eugene J. Soligny, who placed his initials on the lower edge of the medallion with Bryant's portrait. The silver vase was presented to Bryant in a ceremony held on June 20, 1876. It was displayed in the Philadelphia Centennial International Exhibition that year, and in 1877, as the Bryant Testimonial Commission had intended, it entered the collection of the Metropolitan Museum. That it was the first piece of American silver the Metropolitan acquired was appropriate, for Bryant was a founding member of the Museum and served as vice president of its Board of Trustees from 1870 to 1874.

8

AUGUSTUS SAINT-GAUDENS

## 8. Charles F. McKim, Stanford White, and Augustus Saint-Gaudens
1878
Bronze, diam. 6 in. (15.2 cm)
Morris K. Jesup Fund, 1992 (1992.306)

## 9. Charles F. McKim
(fig. 11)
1878
Bronze, 7⅜ x 4⅞ in. (18.7 x 12.4 cm)
Gift of Mrs. Charles D. Norton, 1924 (24.20)

Upon Saint-Gaudens's return to New York in 1875 he met the architects Stanford White (1853–1906) and Charles McKim (1847–1909). The trio enjoyed a fast friendship that blossomed into career-long professional interactions and enduring creative collaborations, sometimes in conjunction with McKim, Mead & White, the most influential architectural firm of America's Gilded Age. First White and later McKim worked with Saint-Gaudens to produce the innovative pedestals and architectural settings for his greatest monuments, among them the Farragut Monument, the *Standing Lincoln*, the Shaw Memorial, and the Sherman Monument (figs. 14, 24, 43, 53).

White and McKim arrived in Paris in summer 1877 ripe for adventure. They convinced Saint-Gaudens, who was toiling away on the Farragut Monument, to join them on a walking tour of southern France in August. The eleven-day "business trip" was filled with high jinks and high adventure, much of it captured in cryptic form on this sketchy medallion. The portraits are arranged like points on a triangle, with White's leonine face at the top, McKim's prematurely balding head with compacted features at the right, and Saint-Gaudens's exaggerated profile to the left. They are surrounded by the tools of their trades (T-square, mallet, and architect's dividers) and the sights they took in (on the left Claus Sluter's Moses Fountain near Dijon and on the right the twelfth-century Romanesque church at Saint-Gilles). Around the irregular edge of the medallion is their itinerary, with the names of the towns they traveled to sometimes upside down, sometimes referred to by first letters only. Saint-Gaudens delighted in such clever allusions in his small, personalized works; that he inscribed *KMA* (kiss my ass) below the T-square is proof that this medallion was originally intended for an audience of three. The Metropolitan's cast belonged to White; it descended in his family until the Museum acquired it in 1992.

The souvenir portrait of McKim, executed shortly after the caricature medallion, was one of a series of noncommissioned portrait reliefs Saint-Gaudens made in Paris for pleasure. This shoulder-length likeness of McKim is more sympathetically proportioned than the one on the medallion, and its compositional elements are tailored to the architect's interests. The inscription in the filleted band below the profile portrait reads, "in souvenir of the ten jolly days passed with you and the illustrious Stanford White in the south of France." Although Saint-Gaudens miscounted the number of days of their trip and misspelled his friend's name as "MacKim," the relief is an affectionate, individualized token. The foliate scroll along the upper border and the group of acanthus leaves at the lower right refer both to McKim's professional calling and to his primary architectural inspiration, the classical.

AUGUSTUS SAINT-GAUDENS

## 10. Francis Davis Millet
1879
Bronze, 10⅝ x 6¾ in. (27 x 17.1 cm)
Gift of Mrs. F. W. Adlard, 1910 (10.223)

Saint-Gaudens met Massachusetts native Francis Davis Millet (1846–1912) in Rome in 1873–74, and their paths crossed frequently over the course of their careers. Both men returned to America in 1875, and both were among the artists assisting John La Farge on mural paintings for Boston's Trinity Church in 1876–77. While Millet considered himself foremost an artist and decorator, he had a secondary career as a writer, in 1877 traveling to Europe as a war correspondent for the *New York Herald* and later penning short stories. He moved easily in international cultural circles and in 1885 settled in the English village of Broadway, which became a gathering place for Anglo-American artists, including John Singer Sargent and Edwin Austin Abbey. Millet's genre paintings of Greco-Roman subjects and English and American historical scenes drew favorable notice.

On March 11, 1879, Saint-Gaudens and Samuel Clemens served as witnesses at Millet's marriage to Elizabeth Greeley Merrill on Montmartre in Paris. This small bas-relief portrait of the groom, dated March 1879, was in all likelihood a wedding present to the newlyweds, for on other occasions Saint-Gaudens presented portraits

10

as wedding gifts (see cat. 22). Millet, calm and modest of mien, is presented in Saint-Gaudens's customary style for portraits of artist-friends, in profile with personalized attributes (in this case, a palette and brushes) and a prominently placed inscription. One of Saint-Gaudens's more frequently replicated reliefs, this particular sand cast bronze was given to the Metropolitan by Millet's daughter in 1910, two years before he died in the sinking of the *Titanic* in April 1912.

AUGUSTUS SAINT-GAUDENS

## 11. *Richard Watson Gilder, Helena de Kay Gilder, and Rodman de Kay Gilder* *(fig. 13)*

1879 (this cast, ca. 1883–84)
Plaster, 8⅝ x 16⅞ in. (21.9 x 42.9 cm)
Gift of David and Joshua Gilder, 2002 (2002.445)

## 12. *Rodman de Kay Gilder*

1879 (this cast, probably 1880)
Bronze, 13½ x 16⅞ in. (34.3 x 42.9 cm)
Purchase, Morris K. Jesup Fund and Mr. and Mrs. Richard J. Schwartz Gift, 1994 (1994.50)

Saint-Gaudens likely met the Gilders in New York in 1875, shortly after his return from Rome. Richard Watson Gilder (1844–1909) was then an editorial assistant at *Scribner's Monthly*, and his wife, Helena

(1846–1916), was a proficient painter and illustrator. The Gilders' Fifteenth Street house was a social locus for avant-garde writers and artists, including Saint-Gaudens, John La Farge, Henry James, and Walt Whitman. Richard Gilder was of inestimable value in launching Saint-Gaudens's career, not only with his propagandistic published writings but also by introducing him to genteel New Yorkers and even serving as a model for the legs for the Farragut statue.

Saint-Gaudens executed this group relief portrait, his first, when the Gilders visited Paris in May 1879. The way he arranged the three figures, with Richard facing Helena and their two-year-old son, Rodman, is particularly resourceful, for it allowed him to retain the easier profile format and avoid the awkward lineup of three figures facing in the same direction. In addition to this plaster version, which dates to about 1883–84 based on a label on the strapping on the back of the wood frame, the Gilders possessed the original bronze cast (now in a private collection and on loan to the Denver Art Museum).

The exceptionally fine bronze cast of young Rodman (1877–1953) also once belonged to the Gilders. Dated September 1879, it was excerpted from the family portrait and slightly modified to give fuller articulation to the hair, now a falling cascade of locks resembling scumbled pigment. The head is surrounded by an undulating background scored all over with wispy etched lines. The free-floating portrait is capped along the upper edge by a cornicelike element, an architectural device often seen in Saint-Gaudens's reliefs that obviates the need for a separate frame.

AUGUSTUS SAINT-GAUDENS

## 13. *Admiral David Glasgow Farragut*

1879–80 (this cast, 1910)
Bronze, 11 x 8 x 8¾ in. (27.9 x 20.3 x 22.2 cm)
Gift by subscription through the Saint-Gaudens Memorial Committee, 1912 (12.76.3a, b)

This bronze bust of Admiral David Glasgow Farragut (1801–1870), the most celebrated naval commander of the Civil War, was cast after the final study Saint-Gaudens made for the monument to Farragut unveiled in New York's Madison Square Park in May 1881 (fig. 14). The study dates to 1879–80, shortly before Saint-Gaudens had the monument cast in bronze at the Gruet foundry in Paris. Farragut's appearance in this bust is nearly the same as in the final statue; the sculptor had fully resolved the piercing glance and resolutely pursed lips that give the admiral his air of authority. The consummate bravado of the richly modeled surface—particularly evident in the tousled hair,

12    13

furrowed brow, and wrinkles around the eyes—is characteristic of the best of Saint-Gaudens's bronzes.

The sculptor's widow, Augusta Saint-Gaudens, copyrighted this bust in January 1908, just months after his death. It was one of many models she cast posthumously from original plasters with the goal of perpetuating her husband's legacy by selling his work to major American museums. The Metropolitan acquired this bronze, along with three others (cats. 15, 29, 32), in 1912 through the auspices of the Saint-Gaudens Memorial Committee, which raised funds to have these replicas cast for the Museum in New York foundries.

14

AUGUSTUS SAINT-GAUDENS
## 14. John Singer Sargent
1880
Bronze, diam. 2½ in. (6.4 cm)
Gift of Mrs. Edward Robinson, 1913 (13.78)

Saint-Gaudens's and John Singer Sargent's remarkable careers developed along parallel tracks. Both prodigiously gifted, they met in Paris in 1877 or 1878 while Saint-Gaudens was at work on his Farragut Monument and Sargent (1856–1925) was studying in the independent atelier of Carolus-Duran and enjoying early success exhibiting his society portraits and genre scenes in the Paris Salons. Sculptor and painter traveled in the same international cosmopolitan circles, sharing not only friends but also patrons. Saint-Gaudens advised Sargent on sculptural elements for his great mural cycle for the Boston Public Library (1890–1916), and after he moved to London in 1886 Sargent reciprocated by introducing Saint-Gaudens to his British colleagues and prospective clients.

This medal, Saint-Gaudens's first, is the smallest of the friendship portraits he completed during his Paris tenure. The likeness of his friend is both matter-of-fact and piercing. The inscription on the grainy-textured field, *BRVTTO RITRATTO*, defies exact interpretation. Literally, it means "crude portrait," which might imply that the sculptor was apologizing for the hasty execution, but "brutto" may also refer to Sargent's forceful and vigorous person, captured on an ironic miniature scale, or it may be an allusion to ancient Roman coins, with their irregular surfaces and profile portrait busts.

The medal was given to the Metropolitan by the wife of Edward Robinson, director of the Museum from 1910 to 1931. The Robinsons were close friends of Sargent's, and they helped the Metropolitan acquire a number of his oils and works on paper, often directly from him.

AUGUSTUS SAINT-GAUDENS
## 15. Jules Bastien-Lepage         (fig. 12)
1880 (this cast, 1910)
Bronze, 14¾ x 10½ in. (37.5 x 26.7 cm)
Gift by subscription through the Saint-Gaudens Memorial Committee, 1912 (12.76.4)

Saint-Gaudens met the French naturalist painter Jules Bastien-Lepage (1848–1884) when they were students at the École des Beaux-Arts in the late 1860s. Although Saint-Gaudens initially disliked Bastien-Lepage, whom he thought overconfident, the two renewed their acquaintance in the late 1870s. As did so many artists of the day, they exchanged artistic tokens of friendship: Bastien-Lepage painted a full-length portrait sketch of Saint-Gaudens (destroyed by fire in 1904), and Saint-Gaudens in turn modeled this low-relief portrait, the last in a series of reliefs he made during his stay in Paris in 1877–80. The half-length format is a departure from his earlier reliefs and presages his more compositionally ambitious commissioned reliefs of the 1880s. The portrait was exhibited in New York in 1881 side-by-side with Bastien-Lepage's painting *Joan of Arc* (1879), which Saint-Gaudens had urged New Yorker Erwin Davis to purchase in 1880 (and which Davis presented to the Metropolitan in 1889).

Bastien-Lepage died from cancer just four years after Saint-Gaudens completed the bas-relief. The portrait became a signature image that Saint-Gaudens frequently exhibited and replicated throughout his career, in a sense as a testament to his departed friend. The Metropolitan's posthumous cast was ordered for the collection through the Saint-Gaudens Memorial Committee in 1910.

AUGUSTUS SAINT-GAUDENS
## 16. The Children of Prescott Hall Butler    (fig. 64)
1880–81 (this carving, 1906–7)
Marble, 24½ x 36 in. (62.2 x 91.4 cm)
Gift of Jacob H. Schiff, 1905 (05.15.1)

Charles Stewart Butler (1876–1954) and Lawrence Smith Butler (1875–1954) are posed as models of filial devotion, holding hands and wearing matching Scottish Highland attire. In the upper left corner an endless interlocking ribbon is inscribed twice with a line from book one of Virgil's *Aeneid*: *DABIT DEVS HIS QVOQVE FINEM* (God will give an end to these also). The composition is testament to Saint-Gaudens's command of low-relief sculpture; the figures overlap to give a sense of three-dimensional depth, but they project forward only slightly.

The boys' father, Prescott Hall Butler, was a prominent New York lawyer who in 1878 hired his Harvard classmate Charles McKim to construct a house, Bytharbor, at Saint James, Long Island. Saint-Gaudens received the commission for this portrait from Stanford White, who was then courting Mrs. Butler's younger sister Bessie Springs Smith (see cat. 22). The original bronze cast (now in a private collection) was a gift from White to Butler (the inscription at the lower left reads, "to my friend Prescott Hall Butler / S / W / sixth of July eighteen hundred and eighty one"). It was installed in a hammered oak frame of White's design and set in the overmantel of the Butlers' dining room. The Metropolitan commissioned this marble version in 1905 (see also cats. 20, 23). It was exhibited alongside the bronze in the 1908 Saint-Gaudens memorial exhibition.

AUGUSTUS SAINT-GAUDENS

## 17. *Samuel Gray Ward* (fig. 19)
1881 (this cast, 1908)
Bronze, 19 x 13¾ in. (48.3 x 34.9 cm)
Gift of Mrs. Augustus Saint-Gaudens, 1912 (12.29)

Samuel Gray Ward (1817–1907), a founder of the Metropolitan Museum and its first treasurer, served on the Board of Trustees from 1870 to 1879. Ward was a financier, a collector of prints, and an intimate of Transcendentalist writers. In 1877 he contracted with McKim, Mead & White to build him a Shingle Style house, Oakwood, in Lenox, Massachusetts. Saint-Gaudens was later introduced to Ward through McKim and White. As the inscription at the top of Ward's portrait attests, Saint-Gaudens completed it in May 1881, an auspicious moment in his career that coincided with the unveiling of the Farragut Monument in Madison Square Park in New York.

Saint-Gaudens evidently felt he could experiment in this, one of his first bas-relief commissions, producing a likeness that remarkably is only an eighth of an inch deep. The freedom of the modeling of the half-length portrait and its spirited vitality make it an exemplar of his command of the sketch aesthetic. In certain passages, such as Ward's hair and the chair back, the surface is drawn rather than modeled. The jacket has a densely mottled appearance, and the background is an allover pattern of tiny horizontal lines. Saint-Gaudens later remarked that *Samuel Gray Ward* was one of the best two or three of his relief portraits. No doubt for this reason, and because of the relationship between the sitter and the Metropolitan, this was the one bronze that Augusta Saint-Gaudens, the sculptor's widow, was persuaded to donate rather than sell to the Museum.

AUGUSTUS SAINT-GAUDENS

## 18. *Vanderbilt Mantelpiece* (fig. 16)
ca. 1881–83
Marble, mosaic, oak, cast iron; 15 ft. 4⅜ in. x 12 ft. 10⅞ in. x 3 ft. 1¼ in.
(4.7 x 3.9 x 1 m)
Gift of Mrs. Cornelius Vanderbilt II, 1925 (25.234)

JOHN LA FARGE (1835–1910), DESIGNER
AUGUSTUS SAINT-GAUDENS, SCULPTOR

## 19. *Vanderbilt Date Panel*
1880–82
Mahogany, ivory, mother-of-pearl, coral; 24½ x 79 in. (62.2 x 200.7 cm)
Gift of Mrs. Cornelius Vanderbilt II, 1925 (25.234b)

This colossal mantelpiece sculpted by Saint-Gaudens was the focal point of the entrance hall to Cornelius Vanderbilt II's house on Fifth Avenue at Fifty-seventh Street in New York, which was constructed by George Browne Post between 1879 and 1882. John La Farge oversaw the sumptuous interior decorative program. La Farge provided the designs for decorative panels for the dining room ceiling that were then executed by Saint-Gaudens, including this inlaid relief panel with the year of the house's completion in Roman numerals. To execute this large decorative project Saint-Gaudens relied on several assistants, including his brother Louis St. Gaudens and young Frederick William MacMonnies.

The mantel is composed primarily of red Numidian marble. Two classically garbed caryatids, Amor and Pax (Love and Peace), support the frieze of carved acanthus-leaf rinceaux. The iron fireback in the hearth, presumably designed by Saint-Gaudens, is decorated with salamanders in flames and a central shield with three acorns (from the family coat of arms) and the monograms of Alice and Cornelius Vanderbilt repeated three times. The mosaic overmantel also has specific Vanderbilt references: The medallion on the left bears the rampant lion of the Vanderbilt crest and the inscription *DEO NON FORTUNA* (By God's grace not fortune's). The right medallion contains the family coat of arms. The classicizing seated woman at the center is holding a garland flanked by beribboned cartouches. She is framed by Latin words of hospitality that may be translated as: "The house at its threshold gives evidence of the master's goodwill. Welcome to the guest who arrives; farewell and helpfulness to him who departs."

When the Vanderbilt house underwent extensive renovations between 1892 and 1894, the date panel was installed above the mantelpiece in the billiard room on the second floor. In 1925, while the house was being razed, Vanderbilt's widow, Alice, presented both the panel and the mantel to the Metropolitan.

AUGUSTUS SAINT-GAUDENS

## 20. *Homer Schiff Saint-Gaudens* (fig. 18)
1882 (this carving, 1906–7)
Marble, 20¼ x 10⅜ in. (51.4 x 26.4 cm)
Gift of Jacob H. Schiff, 1905 (05.15.2)

This sensitive half-length portrait of seventeen-month-old Homer Saint-Gaudens (1880–1958), the Saint-Gaudenses' only child, was modeled in February 1882. The toddler's button nose, full cheeks, and fleshy hand grasping the chair arm underscore Saint-Gaudens's vision of childhood's innocence, which carried through to his other reliefs of early 1880s (see cats. 16, 23). The striated sill gives the vertical low relief a sense of depth, making it appear as if the child is seated in an interior space. The inscription at the top of the portrait notes that it

19

was intended as a gift to Dr. Henry Shiff, Saint-Gaudens's Parisian confidant and his son's namesake (with a variant spelling).

After the sculptor's death Homer Saint-Gaudens edited his father's personal writings and letters, publishing excerpts as the two-volume *Reminiscences of Augustus Saint-Gaudens* in 1913. He worked alongside his mother to found in 1919 the Saint-Gaudens Memorial, which preserved the sculptor's Cornish, New Hampshire, estate and collections (today it operates as the Saint-Gaudens National Historic Site). Homer Saint-Gaudens had a long career in the arts, most notably serving from 1922 to 1950 as the director of the Department of Fine Arts at the Carnegie Institute in Pittsburgh.

A bronze version of this portrait that hung in the sculptor's studio is at the Saint-Gaudens National Historic Site. This marble was carved for the Metropolitan by the Piccirilli Brothers, a Bronx-based firm; Saint-Gaudens's assistant Frances Grimes added finishing touches. Saint-Gaudens was too ill to work at the time and never touched his hand to this or the other two marbles (cats. 16, 23) the Museum commissioned in 1905 with funds from New York financier Jacob H. Schiff.

AUGUSTUS SAINT-GAUDENS

## 21. Mrs. Stanford White (Bessie Springs Smith)
1884 (this carving, by 1888)                                    (fig. 30)
Marble; 25 x 12 in. (63.5 x 30.5 cm), with frame 39½ x 24 in.
(100.3 x 61 cm)
Gift of Erving Wolf Foundation, in memory of Diane R. Wolf, 1976
(1976.388)

## 22. Mrs. Stanford White (Bessie Springs Smith)
1884 (this cast, 1893)
Bronze, diam. 14¼ in. (36.2 cm)
Gift of Anne Tonetti Gugler, 1981 (1981.55.1)

This portrait of Bessie Springs Smith White (1862–1950) was Saint-Gaudens's gift to Stanford White and his bride on the occasion of their wedding on February 7, 1884. Bessie White sat for Saint-Gaudens on several occasions in her bridal finery, and after experimenting with various poses the sculptor arrived at a composition in which she gently lifts her right hand to move the flowing veil off her face. The bunch of rose blooms she holds loosely in her left hand are symbols of love and beauty; in white marble they suggest the bride's purity and youth. The carving of the portrait into marble, financed by Saint-Gaudens to settle a long-standing debt, was completed by 1888, when the marble was exhibited in New York. White then surrounded the bas-relief with an elegant Renaissance Revival tabernacle frame of his design, with an overall floral-and-scroll pattern and a dentil cornice. The portrait remained in the White family until it entered the Metropolitan's collection in 1976. It had been on loan to the Museum on two previous occasions: in 1908 (for the Saint-Gaudens memorial exhibition) and between 1925 and 1940.

22

The circular bronze variant of the marble portrait reflects Saint-Gaudens's somewhat obsessive tendency to explore new compositional possibilities in finished works. Here he has truncated the figure at chest height, eliminating the gown and roses and focusing on the action of the right hand. The reworded inscription, now including the sitter's name, has been moved from the top to the left center. The hair and veil have been reworked with livelier texture, and an ivy vine, an appropriate illusion to wedded love and friendship, winds around the border. This bronze cast was in fact a gift of friendship from Saint-Gaudens to one of his most trusted assistants, Mary Lawrence, who was a distant cousin of Bessie White.

AUGUSTUS SAINT-GAUDENS

## 23. The Children of Jacob H. Schiff                          (fig. 20)
1884–85 (this carving, 1906–7)
Marble, 68⅞ x 51 in. (174.9 x 129.5 cm)
Gift of Jacob H. Schiff, 1905 (05.15.3)

By the mid-1880s Saint-Gaudens's customary portrait relief technique had developed from a low, sketchlike treatment of form to a seamless melding of alto- and bas-relief. This more resolved style is particularly evident in one of his grandest and most complex reliefs, the full-length double portrait of Mortimer Leo Schiff (1877–1931) and Frieda Fanny Schiff (later Warburg; 1876–1958). Framed by two Corinthian pilasters and a frieze decorated with a beribboned garland of blooms and acorns, brother and sister walk hand-in-hand toward the right. They are accompanied by a lanky Scottish deerhound (a cameo appearance by the Saint-Gaudens family pet) that serves both to balance the composition and to increase the sense of depth. The illusion of three dimensionality is enhanced by the deep undercuts at the hem of Frieda's pleated dress and the protrusion of Mortimer's rounded shoe over the edge of the plinth.

The relief was commissioned in 1882 by Sir Ernest Joseph Cassel of London for his childhood friend Jacob H. Schiff, a New York financier and philanthropist (the original bronze is now at the Saint-Gaudens National Historic Site). Saint-Gaudens modeled it in 1884–85 in New York and in Cornish, New Hampshire, during his first summer there. The Metropolitan's marble was one of three portraits of children (see also cats. 16, 20) that Schiff paid to have translated to marble in 1905 for the Museum's developing collection of contemporary American sculpture. The names and ages of the children were inscribed on the original bronze but were omitted from the marble at Schiff's request, for privacy. The date 1888 carved at the base of the marble in Roman numerals is erroneous, for the bronze was cast in 1885 and the marble completed in 1906–7.

AUGUSTUS SAINT-GAUDENS

## 24. Davida Johnson Clark                                     (fig. 37)
1886
Plaster, shellac; 10½ x 6½ x 6½ in. (26.7 x 16.5 x 16.5 cm)
Purchase, Gift of Alice and Evelyn Blight and Mrs. William Payne Thompson, by exchange, 2003 (2003.303)

Saint-Gaudens created this under lifesize portrait of Davida Johnson Clark (1861–1910) as a love token for his model and mistress. The Swedish-born Clark posed for Saint-Gaudens for many years, for such seminal works as *Diana* and *Amor Caritas* (figs. 41, 42, 50). Their relationship spanned more than two decades and in 1889 produced a son, Louis Paul Clark (named for Saint-Gaudens's younger brother).

Saint-Gaudens used this intimate portrait of Clark as a preliminary study for the facial features of *Diana*, his most public of works. Her classic features—aquiline nose with a wide bridge and incised pupils with a calm, faraway look—represent his ideal of female beauty. Her hair is pulled back in a Grecian knot, with spontaneously modeled bangs and the fluid strands at her nape indicated with sweeping incised lines. Her undraped shoulders terminate in a herm format.

This plaster head was painted with shellac to strengthen and waterproof the surface. Saint-Gaudens proclaimed his "horror" of the white plaster versions of his works, and he seldom presented them as gifts, but this head was a highly personal exception (see also fig. 13). It descended in the Clark family until 1987.

25

25, detail

LEONARD WELLS VOLK (1828–1895)

## 25. *Life Mask of Abraham Lincoln*

1860 (this cast, 1886)
Bronze, l. 8 in. (20.3 cm)
Purchase, Jonathan L. Cohen and Allison B. Morrow Gift and Friends of the American Wing Fund, 2007 (2007.185.2)

## 26. *Right Hand of Abraham Lincoln*

1860 (this cast, 1886)
Bronze, l. 6¼ in. (15.9 cm)
Purchase, Jonathan L. Cohen and Allison B. Morrow Gift and Friends of the American Wing Fund, 2007 (2007.185.1)

26

The Chicago sculptor Leonard Wells Volk produced casts of Abraham Lincoln's face and hands in spring 1860. Volk was the first artist to take life molds of Lincoln and to model his portrait, and he made his reputation through a steady output of variant bust portraits of Lincoln based on these life casts. The serene life mask, taken in April in Chicago when the fifty-one-year-old Lincoln (1809–1865) was still beardless, captures his distinctive facial structure and high forehead, large ears, and sunken cheeks. Absent are any hints of the passionate rhetoric and tousled appearance with which he is typically associated. The eyes are blank, as they were not covered in plaster during the hour-long molding process. Volk took the molds for the hands on May 20, 1860, at Lincoln's house in Springfield, Illinois, two days after he was nominated for president at the Republican National Convention. Lincoln's right hand, with its prominent veins, appears swollen because of the many congratulatory handshakes. It is noticeably larger than the cast of his left hand, which is also in the shape of a fist (an example is in the New-York Historical Society). Volk suggested that he hold something in his right hand to resemble a document, so Lincoln sawed off the end of a broom handle and used that.

In 1886 Volk's son Douglas sold the original plaster casts of Lincoln's face and hands to Saint-Gaudens, journalist Richard Watson Gilder, and collectors Thomas B. Clarke and Erwin Davis. In order to finance the $1,500 purchase of these hallowed casts, the men initiated a fund whereby subscribers would receive a set of replicas (in bronze for an $85 contribution, in plaster for $50). Thirty individuals and three institutions subscribed, and in 1888 the original plasters and a set of bronze replicas were donated to the U.S. government (they are now in the National Museum of American History, Smithsonian

Institution). The program of casting was overseen by Saint-Gaudens, who added dedicatory inscriptions in his distinctive lettering style of capitalized words punctuated by bullets. Each bronze mask was dated February 1886 and individualized by inserting the subscriber's name in an inscription noting that he was "a subscriber to the fund for the purchase and presentation to the United States government of the original mask made in Chicago April 1860 by Leonard W. Volk from the living face of Abraham Lincoln." The Metropolitan's face and right hand belong to the set originally owned by Gilder. Saint-Gaudens later recalled that Gilder's cast of the face was one of the best in quality.

The appearance of the original casts of Lincoln's face and hands was timely, for Saint-Gaudens was then immersed in modeling the *Standing Lincoln* (1884–87; figs. 23, 24) for Chicago's Lincoln Park. For Saint-Gaudens, capturing a convincingly realistic likeness was paramount, so these casts were significant reference points for that sculpture and his *Seated Lincoln* (1897–1906) for Chicago's Grant Park. These first-generation casts and the many subsequent *surmoulages* (duplicate casts) have served as the basis for untold numbers of painted and sculpted portraits of Lincoln in his many guises: rail-splitter, statesman, Great Emancipator, and martyr.

27

AUGUSTUS SAINT-GAUDENS

## 27. The Puritan

1883–86 (this cast, 1899 or after)
Bronze, 30½ x 18½ x 13 in. (77.5 x 47 x 33 cm)
Bequest of Jacob Ruppert, 1939 (39.65.53)

STANFORD WHITE (1853–1906)

## 28. Sketch of Saint-Gaudens's Statue of Deacon Samuel Chapin, Springfield, Massachusetts    (fig. 27)

ca. 1887
Pastel, charcoal, and pencil on paper; 12 x 18⅛ in. (30.5 x 46 cm)
Morris K. Jesup Fund, 1999 (1999.249)

*The Puritan* was dedicated on Thanksgiving Day, 1887, in Stearns Square in Springfield, Massachusetts. For this monument to Deacon Samuel Chapin (1598–1675), one of the city's early settlers, Saint-Gaudens again partnered with Stanford White to produce a custom-designed base and landscaped environment for the bronze sculpture. White plotted out his sketch for the statue's setting with a straight-edge, delineating an outer pathway as well as one with a bench that crosses in front of the sculpture. The drawing is otherwise rendered in quick strokes and shadings to indicate trees, hedges, and a fountain with a central sphere. Areas of water, grass, leaves, and sky are colored with pastels. The final result featured the same major elements, with the addition of brick pathways that led the viewer around the fountain and to the sculpture. (The monument, with only the red granite base, was relocated in 1899 to Springfield's Merrick Park.)

When Saint-Gaudens began reducing and casting his sculptures for commercial distribution in the early 1890s, he recognized the potential appeal of *The Puritan* and its embodiment of old New

England values. His move abroad in 1897 finally spurred the reduction and casting of *Puritan* statuettes in Parisian foundries late the following year. These differ from the original monument in that a second pine branch and the inscription *THE PVRITAN* have been added to the base. Casts were marketed in Boston and New York showrooms both before and after Saint-Gaudens returned to the United States in 1900. Following his death in 1907 his widow, Augusta, continued to produce good-quality castings that in the absence of foundry marks can be nearly indistinguishable from those made in his lifetime. Documented casts of *The Puritan* number more than forty, making it Saint-Gaudens's most commercially successful statuette.

AUGUSTUS SAINT-GAUDENS

## 29. Robert Louis Stevenson    (fig. 34)

1887–88 (this cast, 1910)
Bronze, diam. 35¼ in. (89.5 cm)
Gift by subscription through the Saint-Gaudens Memorial Committee, 1912 (12.76.1)

## 30. Robert Louis Stevenson

1887–88 (this cast, 1898)
Bronze, diam. 17⅞ in. (45.4 cm)
Gift of Anne Tonetti Gugler, in memory of her mother, Mary Lawrence Tonetti, 1981 (1981.55.2)

Scottish-born Robert Louis Stevenson (1850–1894) produced a string of best-selling books in the 1880s that included *New Arabian Nights* (1882), *Treasure Island* (1883), and *Kidnapped* (1886). Among his American admirers was Saint-Gaudens, who seized the opportunity to model a noncommissioned bas-relief portrait when Stevenson arrived in New York in fall 1887. He modeled the delicate profile head with ease, but it was not until the following spring during sittings in Manasquan, New Jersey, that he developed a satisfactory pose. The solution, originally horizontal but soon switched to a tondo format, presents Stevenson reclining against pillows, his knees pulled up, with papers in one hand and a cigarette in the other. It was true to life, as the tubercular author frequently wrote in bed. The prominent inscription on the relief's expansive field is Stevenson's poem "To Will H. Low." (Low, an artist, was a mutual friend who had arranged the sittings.) During the sittings a warm relationship developed between Stevenson and the "God-like sculptor," as he called Saint-Gaudens. Around the medallion's border is an ivy-and-berry motif signifying friendship.

Stevenson's American visit and his death in Samoa in 1894 at the age of forty-four were closely followed by the national press, and Saint-Gaudens capitalized on the writer's notoriety. Beginning in 1890 he cast thirty-six-inch versions of Stevenson's medallion (including one he sent to Stevenson in Samoa). About 1895 he made reduced versions,

30

approximately eighteen and twelve inches in diameter, for unlimited serial issue. The three variant sizes were cast in French and American foundries, and a rectangular version was available after 1902. In 1904 a large rectangular version, with compositional modifications, was unveiled as Stevenson's memorial in Saint Giles' Cathedral in Edinburgh. By far Saint-Gaudens's most frequently cast relief portrait, it continued to be produced after his death.

Saint-Gaudens strove to maintain the integrity of each individual bronze of the Stevenson medallion and to avoid the appearance of mass production. By cutting out and replacing sections of the plaster models he changed the presentation of the inscription, the arrangement of the bedcovers, the number of pillows, and the top of the bedpost. The Metropolitan's thirty-six-inch version (actually 35¼ inches in diameter) was ordered by the Saint-Gaudens Memorial Committee and cast by Tiffany Studios in 1910; it has a custom inscription, "REPLICA MADE FOR THE METROPOLITAN MUSEUM OF ART ASPET MCMX," rather than the usual dedication to Stevenson. Saint-Gaudens presented the eighteen-inch cast to his studio assistant Mary Lawrence as a Christmas present in 1898. It retains a quarter-sawed poplar surround with a beadwork opening and three rosettes that was frequently used for smaller Stevenson reliefs.

AUGUSTUS SAINT-GAUDENS

### 31. *Frances Folsom Cleveland*
1887–92 (this cast, 1902)
Bronze, diam. 5½ in. (14 cm)
Purchase, Friends of the American Wing Fund, 2008 (2008.156)

In June 1886 President Grover Cleveland wed Frances Folsom (1864–1947) in a White House ceremony. The beautiful Mrs. Cleveland, twenty-seven years her husband's junior, was the daughter of his late law partner, Oscar Folsom. In summer 1887 she visited their close friends Helena and Richard Gilder at their summer home on Buzzard's Bay in Marion, Massachusetts. Saint-Gaudens, also a guest, modeled the relief portrait in the Gilders' studio. The sittings took place over a period of three weeks in August (see fig. 32).

Although Saint-Gaudens was fond of Mrs. Cleveland, he found her a difficult sitter and lingered over the portrait. By 1892 he had finally completed a seventeen-inch medallion that depicts her at shoulder length in three-quarter profile, so that her nose is almost three-dimensional. She wears an upswept hairstyle, a fashionable dress with a high collar, and a beaded necklace. In late 1901 Saint-Gaudens reduced the scale of the plaster medallion to five-and-a-half

inches in diameter, and early in 1902 he cast it in bronze. One cast (the Metropolitan's) was given to Richard Watson Gilder as a birthday present; the other, presented to the sitter, remains in the Cleveland family. In 1907, when Frances Cleveland arranged to lend her cast to the memorial exhibition at the Metropolitan,

31

she observed to Daniel Chester French that while she did not think the likeness particularly suggested her, it certainly suggested Saint-Gaudens.

AUGUSTUS SAINT-GAUDENS

### 32. *General William Tecumseh Sherman*          (fig. 45)
1888 (this cast, 1910)
Bronze, 31¼ x 21½ x 12½ in. (79.4 x 54.6 x 31.8 cm)
Gift by subscription through the Saint-Gaudens Memorial Committee, 1912 (12.76.2)

General William Tecumseh Sherman (1820–1891), venerated by the Union cause and vilified by the Confederate one, is remembered as a brilliant, if controversial, tactician and longtime commanding general of the United States Army. After he had retired from active duty and relocated to New York in 1886, Sherman was frequently asked to sit for his portrait, a prospect he resisted. Saint-Gaudens's successful entrée came about through Whitelaw Reid, editor of the *New York Daily Tribune*, and Sherman's daughter Rachel. During some eighteen two-hour sessions between January and March 1888, the general was a feisty and entertaining sitter. In his *Reminiscences* Saint-Gaudens wrote that his likeness of Sherman was based on his boyhood vision of him as a typical American soldier. The final result, however, projects the aura of authority and pride of a seasoned and celebrated general.

Sherman's robust lifesize likeness is among the most consummately realistic of Saint-Gaudens's portraits, its bronze surface tactile, fluid, and practically pulsating with detail, from the furrowed brows and weathered face to the hard-set jaw. The general is dressed in military uniform, his steely independent streak reflected by the askew bowtie that he apparently refused to straighten during the sittings. The bust rests on a block inscribed with his name that itself surmounts a pillow of laurel leaves bound by ribbon, with a larger plinth below.

Sherman's satisfaction with the portrait ensured for Saint-Gaudens the plum commission for an equestrian statue of the general for New York. The commission was awarded to him in 1892, the year after Sherman's death, and the gilded monument was unveiled in 1903 in Grand Army Plaza, at Fifth Avenue and Fifty-ninth Street (fig. 53). Saint-Gaudens brought a plaster version of this naturalistic bust to Paris to serve as the basis for the monument. The bust was selected for the Metropolitan by the Saint-Gaudens Memorial Committee, no doubt because of the proximity of the monument to the Museum. It also was considered a pendant of sorts to the bust of Admiral David Glasgow Farragut (cat. 13) cast after Saint-Gaudens's final study for his other great Civil War monument in New York (fig. 14).

AUGUSTUS SAINT-GAUDENS

### 33. *Mrs. Schuyler Van Rensselaer (Mariana Griswold)*
1888 (this cast, 1890)                                       (fig. 31)
Bronze; 20⅜ x 7¾ in. (51.8 x 19.7 cm), with frame 34¾ x 16½ in.
(88.3 x 41.9 cm)
Gift of Mrs. Schuyler Van Rensselaer, 1917 (17.104)

Mariana Griswold Van Rensselaer (1851–1934), influential Gilded Age author, critic, and reformer, was one of Saint-Gaudens's most loyal advocates during his rise to success in the 1880s. After her positive response to the Farragut Monument (fig. 14) in 1881, she championed his sculptures in such prominent journals as *Century Magazine* and *American Architect and Building News*. In 1886 an illustration of Saint-Gaudens's classicizing central angel for the Morgan family tomb in Cedar Hill Cemetery in Hartford, Connecticut (destroyed by fire in 1884, before it was completed) was printed on the title page of her *Book of American Figure Painters* (fig. 48). Saint-Gaudens and Van Rensselaer were also devoted friends, and this elegant likeness may have been a tangible thank-you for her salutary article in the *Century* on the *Standing Lincoln* (fig. 24) after its unveiling in 1887.

Aesthetically, this bronze reflects Saint-Gaudens's bas-relief technique at its most refined: a head of distinguished bearing; confident, spontaneous modeling in the curled locks of hair and the blouse with a high ruffled collar; undulating, striated background; and deep undercutting at the shoulders to suggest depth. Saint-Gaudens posed his sitter in left-facing profile within an elongated vertical format. The Latin inscription at the top, *ANIMVS NON OPVS* (The spirit, not the work), refers to Van Rensselaer's idealistic aesthetic beliefs. The rosettes at the bottom are echoed in the carved oak frame, a harmonious design of scalloped shell, foliated cornucopia, and egg-and-dart beadwork designed by Stanford White.

Van Rensselaer lent this sand cast, a superlative example of American foundry work, to the five-city tour of the Saint-Gaudens memorial exhibition from 1908 to 1910.

### AUGUSTUS SAINT-GAUDENS
### PHILIP MARTINY (1858–1927)

### 34–35. *Two Examples of the George Washington Inaugural Centennial Medal* *(fig. 62)*
1889
Bronze, diam. of each 4½ in. (11.4 cm)
Gift of Henry G. Marquand, 1890 (90.18.1, 2)

In winter 1888–89 Saint-Gaudens received his first official medallic commission, from the Committee on Art and Exhibition of the Washington Centennial Celebration. The medal was to be the official souvenir for the centennial of George Washington's swearing-in as first president of the United States on April 30, 1789, at New York's Federal Hall.

Although he designed the medal, Saint-Gaudens turned its modeling over to his assistant Philip Martiny. The half-length profile portrait of Washington in Continental uniform on the front face of the medal harks back to the authoritative sculptural portrayal of the *pater patriae* by Jean Antoine Houdon, the full-length marble statue of 1792 in the State Capitol in Richmond, Virginia, which was in turn based on a life portrait from 1785. At the right are the fasces of majesty, the bundle of staves representing the United States and the axe and blade its military and executive power. Thirteen stars symbolizing the original states are evenly spaced near the edge. On the reverse, an American eagle with spread wings and arrows and an olive branch in its claws bears a shield with the inscription *E PLVRIBVS VNVM* (Out of many, one). At the lower left are a lengthy commemorative inscription and the shield of arms of New York City. Around the border are thirty-eight stars representing the states in the Union in April 1889. The medal's compositional format and technique are strongly indebted to the Renaissance medallic art Saint-Gaudens admired. (He collected plaster casts after Pisanello to display in his studio.)

The medal was cast by Gorham Manufacturing Company in an edition of 2,000 bronze and 10 silver examples. Henry Gurdon Marquand, chairman of the Washington Centennial Committee on Art and Exhibition and president of The Metropolitan Museum of Art, donated these two bronzes to the Museum in 1890. They were the first works by Saint-Gaudens to enter the collection.

### AUGUSTUS SAINT-GAUDENS

### 36. *World's Columbian Exposition Commemorative Presentation Medal*
1892–94 (this cast, by 1896)
Bronze, diam. 3 in. (7.6 cm)
Morris K. Jesup Fund, 1995 (1995.4)

The World's Columbian Exposition, held in Chicago between May and October 1893 to celebrate the four-hundredth anniversary of Christopher Columbus's landing in America, heralded American technological, social, and artistic progress on a grand civic scale and was visited by some twenty-six million people. Saint-Gaudens, who served as an advisor for the sculptural program, also accepted the commission for the official award medal.

Saint-Gaudens had completed his design for the medal by the time of the fair's closing. His design for the obverse met ready acceptance. It shows Columbus alighting on the shores of the New World. At the lower right are three male figures, one bearing an unfurling banner, and above them are the symbolic Pillars of Hercules with the three Spanish caravels and the inscription *PLVS VLTRA*. His concept for the reverse, however—a nude male youth representing the Spirit of America—was deemed improper by the United States Senate Quadro-Centennial Committee. Two variant designs with the figure's genitals covered and a third with a wreath-encircled eagle and inscription were also rejected. In the end, Saint-Gaudens's obverse was muled with a design for the reverse by Charles E. Barber (1840–1917), longtime chief

36, obverse

engraver at the United States Mint. Disgusted, Saint-Gaudens viewed Barber as his career-long nemesis, especially during his later work on designs for U.S. coins (see cats. 48, 49).

The reverse of the final minted version of the medal features a central tablet with an inscription and a space for a drop-in die with the name of the recipient. The tablet is flanked by flaming torches symbolizing light or intelligence, and below it the *Santa Maria* appears at full sail. Above, two winged (and ironically bare-breasted) females hold symbolic attributes— a trumpet and laurel wreaths and a stylus and a blank tablet—that celebrate the award recipient. The hubs and dies for the medal were produced at the United States Mint in Philadelphia and farmed out for striking

36, reverse

to the Scovill Manufacturing Company of Waterbury, Connecticut. The medal was finally awarded to recipients in 1896. The Metropolitan's example retains its original velvet-lined aluminum case.

AUGUSTUS SAINT-GAUDENS

### 37. *Diana*
1892–93 (this cast, 1928)
Bronze, gilt; 101¾ x 53½ x 14⅛ in. (258.4 x 135.9 x 35.9 cm)
Rogers Fund, 1928 (28.101)

### 38. *Diana*      *(fig. 42)*
1893–94 (this cast, 1894 or after)
Bronze, 28¼ x 16¼ x 14 in. (71.8 x 41.3 x 35.6 cm)
Gift of Lincoln Kirstein, 1985 (1985.353)

These two versions of *Diana*, Saint-Gaudens's only female nude, originate from the figure he sculpted for the top of the tower on the Madison Square Garden building designed by Stanford White and completed in 1890 (see fig. 36). Diana, Roman goddess of the hunt and of the moon, was an apt subject for a palace of sport. The eighteen-foot sheet copper version (fig. 39), erected in 1891, was deemed too large by White and Saint-Gaudens and removed in 1892. A year later a second version, a more graceful thirteen feet high (see fig. 40), was installed, and it dominated the New York skyline until 1925, when the building was razed. Despite strenuous efforts to keep *Diana* on display in New York (one of the proposed locations was atop a tower of the Manhattan Bridge), in 1932 the sculpture entered the collection of the Philadelphia Museum of Art (see fig. 41). The Metropolitan's gilded *Diana* was cast

37

for the collection in 1928. Daniel Chester French, Museum trustee and head of its Committee on Sculpture, civic-mindedly pushed for its acquisition so that a version of *Diana* would be kept in New York's public eye. The resulting six-and-a-half-foot gilded bronze version is a half-size model of the thirteen-foot *Diana*. It was cast from a mold taken off a Portland cement cast that Saint-Gaudens presented to White in 1894 and that White installed on the grounds of Box Hill, his home in Saint James, Long Island.

The smaller *Diana* statuette, also reduced after the thirteen-foot version, represents one of three editions Saint-Gaudens created during the 1890s. In this version, cast in Paris, the elegant, streamlined figure is posed on tiptoe on a sphere set on a two-tier base with dentil molding. This superlative cast is distinguished by the delicate chasing to the hair and face and the matte gold patina, the result of electroplating gold, copper, and tin to the bronze surface.

AUGUSTUS SAINT-GAUDENS

### 39. *Louise Adele Gould*
1893 (this carving, 1894)
Marble, 40¾ x 25½ in. (103.5 x 64.8 cm)
Gift of Charles W. Gould, 1915 (15.105.1)

### 40. *Louise Adele Gould*
1894 (this carving, 1895)
Marble, 22 x 15½ x 10 in. (55.9 x 39.4 x 25.4 cm)
Gift of Charles W. Gould, 1915 (15.105.2)

### 41. *Louise Adele Gould*      *(fig. 68)*
1904
Marble, 16½ x 17 x 4½ in. (41.9 x 43.2 x 11.4 cm)
Bequest of Charles W. Gould, 1931 (32.62.1)

This trio of posthumous portraits represent Louise Adele Dickerson Gould, who died suddenly in 1883 at the age of twenty-six, less than three years after her marriage to New York lawyer Charles Gould. In 1893 Gould commissioned Saint-Gaudens to model a bust-length medallion portrait of his wife, based on a photograph, depicting her in her wedding gown and veil. Stanford White advised Saint-Gaudens on the design for the integral marble frame evoking a tombstone. The inscription on the frame underscores the reverence of the bereaved husband, who never remarried, for his departed wife.

Pleased with the first portrait, Gould ordered a marble bust terminated by a socle base in which his wife appears sweetly pious in a classicizing drapery held by knots at her shoulders. Playing to Saint-Gaudens's love of technical experimentation, Gould suggested that he produce wax casts. Saint-Gaudens extended the shoulder and terminated the portrait horizontally below the shoulders, in the manner of quattrocento busts. The sculptor's Cornish colleague Herbert Adams, who specialized in polychrome sculptures, tinted one of the casts to produce a startlingly lifelike vision of the sitter (now in a private collection). In 1904 Gould ordered another version of the bust, in this horizontal format. Although the features faithfully replicate the earlier bust, the drapery at the shoulders has been slightly modified. The white marble bust surmounts a three-and-a-half-inch base of variegated yellow marble of Italian origin.

39

40

All three marbles were cut by the Piccirilli Brothers in the Bronx, then the foremost American carving studio. Gould gave the first and second portraits of his wife to the Museum in 1915, the year he was elected a trustee. He retained the third, the one he considered the most beautiful, until his death in 1931.

AUGUSTUS SAINT-GAUDENS

## 42. *Amor Caritas* (fig. 50)
1880–98 (this cast, 1918)
Bronze, gilt; 103¼ x 50 in. (262.3 x 127 cm)
Rogers Fund, 1918 (19.124)

The classicizing female was a leitmotif in Saint-Gaudens's oeuvre, a fitting foil to his vibrant monuments to Civil War heroes. Occasionally the sculptor combined the allegorical (female) with the real (male) in a unified statement, as in the Shaw and Sherman monuments (figs. 43, 53), yet just as often he modeled his full-size ideal figure in a frontal pose with flowing gown and serene demeanor. Beginning in 1879 he experimented with three freestanding draped figures for the tomb of the Edwin D. Morgan family in Cedar Hill Cemetery in Hartford, Connecticut (which was only partially completed when it was destroyed by fire in 1884). These were followed in 1881–83 by the caryatids Amor and Pax for the mantelpiece in the entrance hall of the Cornelius Vanderbilt II house (fig. 16) and in 1887 by the winged figure for the tomb of Ann Maria Smith in Island Cemetery in Newport, Rhode Island. But Saint-Gaudens's ideal female reached her ultimate state of refinement in *Amor Caritas*, who stands upon a semicircular plinth with proud, upright bearing. For the acanthus-ornamented tablet the angel holds aloft between her sensuously curving wings, Saint-Gaudens considered several titles, including *To Know Is to Forgive, Peace on Earth, God Is Love*, and *Good Will towards Man*, before selecting *Amor Caritas* (Love [and] Charity). In 1902 Saint-Gaudens produced a modified version of *Amor Caritas* in stone for the Maria Mitchell Memorial in Saint Stephen's Church in Philadelphia (now in the Philadelphia Museum of Art). In all its variants, the sculpture's symbolism is arguably less spiritual than meditative upon such positive universal themes as love, peace, and redemption.

Upon completing his large version of *Amor Caritas* in Paris in 1898, Saint-Gaudens moved purposefully to produce forty-inch-high reductions. First cast in Paris in 1899, the smaller statues enjoyed commercial success. That first year the Musée du Luxembourg purchased a full-size bronze cast (now Musée d'Orsay, Paris), a supreme honor for Saint-Gaudens. The Museum's cast was commissioned from the artist's widow in 1918. According to trustee Daniel Chester French, its original patina was intended as "'mat' gold and not bright."

AUGUSTUS SAINT-GAUDENS

## 43. *Josephine Shaw Lowell*
1899 (this carving, 1901)
Marble, 16 x 9¼ in. (40.6 x 23.5 cm)
Gift of Charles C. Burlingham, 1925 (25.89)

Josephine Shaw Lowell (1843–1905) was a prominent reformer in health, poverty, prisoner, and labor causes, in 1882 founding the Charity Organization Society in New York, which now operates as the Community Service Society. Lowell was the older sister of Colonel Robert Gould Shaw, and she and Saint-Gaudens became acquainted during the years (1884–97) that he was working on her brother's memorial for Boston Common (see fig. 43). Her husband, Colonel Charles Russell Lowell, also perished in the Civil War.

Lowell sat for Saint-Gaudens in Paris in 1899, while he was in the midst of modeling the heroic-size Sherman Monument (fig. 53). The rendering of her facial features on the low-relief portrait is matter-of-fact, but her fichu with its ruffled lace edge and the delicate wisps

43

escaping her upswept hairstyle were handled with the sculptor's characteristic fluency. Below the chest-length portrait is an ornamental tablet with the date 1899 in Roman numerals surrounded by acanthus leaves, beadwork, and simple molding. The rest of the background is unadorned save for Saint-Gaudens's characteristic monogram cipher. Pleased with the result, Lowell ordered this marble replica, which was carved by Annette St. Gaudens, wife of the sculptor's brother Louis St. Gaudens. In 1925 New York lawyer Charles C. Burlingham, a friend of both the artist and the sitter, purchased the portrait from the estate of Lowell's daughter, Carlotta Russell Lowell, and presented it to the Metropolitan.

AUGUSTUS SAINT-GAUDENS

## 44. *Victory* (fig. 47)

1892–1903 (this cast, 1914 or after, by 1916)
Bronze, gilt; 38 x 9½ x 18½ in. (96.5 x 24.1 x 47 cm)
Rogers Fund, 1917 (17.90.1)

## 45. *Head of Victory* (fig. 63)

1897–1903 (this cast, 1907)
Bronze, 8 x 7 x 6½ in. (20.3 x 17.8 x 16.5 cm)
Rogers Fund, 1907 (07.90)

This statuette of Victory was reduced after the full-size figure leading General Sherman on horseback in the monument to him in Grand Army Plaza in New York (fig. 53). Saint-Gaudens conceived the winged allegorical female as part of the overall design from the start, but it was not until 1897 that he concentrated on modeling the forward-

moving figure and flowing draperies. Victory surges ahead in a gown emblazoned with an American eagle, brandishing a palm branch. Although the sculptor considered reducing the group following the unveiling of the Sherman Monument in 1903, it was not until 1911 that Augusta Saint-Gaudens, his widow, reached an agreement with his master molder, Gaëtan Ardisson, to do so. Gilded bronze reductions went into production at the Gorham Manufacturing Company in Providence, Rhode Island, in 1912.

Saint-Gaudens began producing bronze casts of the *Head of Victory* in 1902, and they were sold in an unlimited edition before and after his death. Because he returned to an earlier, unused study for this head, it differs from the final head of Victory on the Sherman Monument. To the termination of the bust Saint-Gaudens added a tablet inscribed *NIKH-EIPHNH* (Victory-Peace), reiterating his stated symbolism for the Victory figure in the Sherman Monument. The Metropolitan's cast entered the collection shortly before Saint-Gaudens's death, so the sculptor was able to advise trustee Daniel Chester French and the Gorham foundry on its surface appearance.

AUGUSTUS SAINT-GAUDENS
ADOLPH ALEXANDER WEINMAN (1870–1952)

## 46. *Theodore Roosevelt Special Inaugural Medal*

1905 (fig. 54)
Bronze, diam. 2⅞ in. (7.4 cm)
Morris K. Jesup Fund, 2008 (2008.112)

Saint-Gaudens's and Theodore Roosevelt's mutual quest to produce coins as worthy and beautiful as those from ancient times (see also cats. 48, 49) had its first tangible result in this special medal celebrating the president's inauguration to his second term in March 1905. The Inaugural Committee contracted with Joseph K. Davison's Sons to issue an official commemorative medal designed by Charles E. Barber and George Morgan in an edition of 3,000. But Roosevelt, dissatisfied with the design, also requested that Saint-Gaudens complete a special inaugural version that would meet his (Roosevelt's) own exacting artistic standards.

Saint-Gaudens designed and offered creative guidance on this important commission while leaving the modeling to his former assistant Adolph Alexander Weinman. On the obverse is a forthright and realistic profile head of Roosevelt (1858–1919) facing left with a dedicatory legend above and below. To the right is the Latin motto *AEQVVM CVIQVE*, or "to each what is equitable," a loose interpretation of Roosevelt's campaign slogan "a square deal for every man," which was felt to be too colloquial to inscribe on a medal. On the reverse is an eagle posed in ancient Egyptian Ptolemaic style, facing left upon a craggy rock, powerful and proud in its bearing. It is flanked by the motto of the Seal of the United States, *E PLVRIBVS VNVM* (Out of many, one). The dual monogram cipher on the rock ledge below the eagle memorializes Saint-Gaudens's acknowledgment that Weinman deserved equal recognition.

The medal was cast by Tiffany & Co. in spring 1905 in an edition of 120 bronze and 2 gold examples (5 bronzes and 1 gold were cast subsequently). The Metropolitan's medal, with its splendid golden brown patina, was one of 35 appropriated to Roosevelt by the Inaugural Committee for his personal distribution. Roosevelt gave this medal to Charles A. Boynton, then the White House reporter for the Associated Press, and it remained in the Boynton family until shortly before its acquisition by the Metropolitan.

48, obverse and reverse

49, obverse and reverse

AUGUSTUS SAINT-GAUDENS

## 47. Cornish Celebration Presentation Plaquette

1905–6 *(fig. 60)*
Bronze, silver; 3¼ x 1¾ in. (8.3 x 4.5 cm)
Gift of Kenyon Cox, 1908 (08.216)

On the evening of June 22, 1905, Saint-Gaudens's twenty years in Cornish, New Hampshire, were marked by a celebratory tribute in the form of an elaborately planned open-air play titled "A Masque of 'Ours': The Gods and the Golden Bowl." The pageant was written by Louis Shipman; the music was composed by Arthur Whiting and performed by members of the Boston Symphony Orchestra. Among the many Cornish Colony residents, young and old, who assumed the roles of mythical gods and goddesses were painter Maxfield Parrish, who created the actors' masks and played the role of the centaur Chiron, and Saint-Gaudens's assistant Frances Grimes, who delivered the prologue as Iris, messenger of the gods. Other notable players were architect Charles Platt, painter Everett Shinn, and poet Percy MacKaye.

Saint-Gaudens's pleasure at this *fête champêtre*, as he called it, resulted in his modeling an affectionate tribute to the masque participants in the form of silvered plaquettes struck in Paris and distributed during the summer of 1906 (the playwright, Shipman, received a large gilded bronze version that is now in a private collection). The classicizing design, topped by the golden bowl presented to Saint-Gaudens at the end of the play, re-creates the Arcadian setting of the masque—curtained trees flanking a columned temple with a lighted altar. Winged Amor appears on the temple steps with a lyre. On the pediment above and the plinth below Saint-Gaudens painstakingly listed the names of all the participants in the masque, and the back of each plaquette was inscribed with the individual recipient's name.

Saint-Gaudens's good friend the painter Kenyon Cox (see cat. 51), a member of the committee for the memorial exhibition held at the Metropolitan in 1908, presented his plaquette to the Museum that year.

AUGUSTUS SAINT-GAUDENS

## 48. United States Ten-dollar Gold Piece

1906–7 (this coin, 1910)
Gold, diam. 1⅛ in. (2.7 cm)
Gift of Heinz L. Stoppelmann, 1979 (1979.486.6)

## 49. United States Twenty-dollar Gold Piece

1905–7 (this coin, 1911)
Gold, diam. 1¼ in. (3.3 cm)
Gift of Heinz L. Stoppelmann, 1979 (1979.486.8)

Having proclaimed the coinage produced by the United States Mint uninspired and commonplace, President Theodore Roosevelt invited Saint-Gaudens to redesign the ten- and twenty-dollar gold coins and the one-cent piece. Some ten months later, in November 1905, Saint-Gaudens submitted his preliminary sketches, becoming the first artist unaffiliated with the Mint to design a regular coinage issue. Roosevelt later declared the resulting coins (his "pet crime") more beautiful than any since the days of the ancient Greeks.

The obverse of the twenty-dollar piece, or double eagle, depicts the dynamic figure of Liberty, derived from Saint-Gaudens's Victory from the Sherman Monument (see cat. 44, fig. 53). To her right is the U. S.

Capitol, and behind her rays of sun, symbolizing enlightenment, burst upward. On the reverse is a soaring eagle inspired by the eagle on the 1857 and 1858 U.S. pennies. For the obverse of the ten-dollar piece, the eagle, Saint-Gaudens used the head of Liberty wearing a feather headdress. The reverse has a standing eagle similar to the one used on the Theodore Roosevelt Special Inaugural Medal (cat. 46, fig. 54). Saint-Gaudens completed numerous sketches for these designs and then guided his studio assistant Henry Hering as he carried out the finished models.

Saint-Gaudens died in August 1907, just before the gold coins were minted for circulation. (Roosevelt had ordered that they be put into circulation before the start of 1908.) The ten-dollar coins were minted first, and the twenty-dollar coins followed by mid-December. Both coins were minted in Denver, as the *D* on their obverse faces signifies. The outstanding early versions (see figs. 55, 56) are notable for their wire rims and high degree of relief, which prevented them from being stacked and required many strikes to achieve the final result. The Metropolitan's examples are business strikes after designs modified by Charles E. Barber, chief engraver of the U.S. Mint, to adapt them for commercial use (creating the flattened relief required just one blow of the press). They contain the motto "In God We Trust," which was eliminated from the earliest versions but ordered to appear on all coins struck after July 1, 1908.

The one-cent piece for which Saint-Gaudens prepared models was never minted.

LOUIS ST. GAUDENS (1854–1913)

## 50. Benjamin Franklin Commemorative Medal

1906
Bronze, diam. 4 in. (10.2 cm)
Gift of President Theodore Roosevelt, 1906 (06.1192)

From the early 1870s onward Saint-Gaudens's younger brother Louis, who preferred to spell his last name "St. Gaudens," was a frequent contributor to the Saint-Gaudens studio enterprise. He collaborated on such large-scale projects as the decorations for the Cornelius Vanderbilt II house (see cats. 18, 19), while also maintaining an active independent career, primarily creating architectural sculpture for East

50, obverse and reverse

Coast cities. From time to time Augustus passed along to Louis commissions like this medal to commemorate the bicentennial of Benjamin Franklin's birth. The commission, brought about by an Act of Congress of April 27, 1904, was originally awarded to Augustus, and he continued to negotiate with the organizing committee, but he insisted that Louis sign the work as his own.

In 1905, through the auspices of Metropolitan trustee Daniel Chester French, Saint-Gaudens received a plaster copy of Jean-Antoine Houdon's marble bust of Benjamin Franklin (1788), which had been given to the Museum in 1872. This well-known portrait was the reference point for the bust-length profile on the medal's obverse. The reverse depicts a classically garbed figure of History sitting upon her throne holding a shield with a Latin inscription that translates as: "He snatched from the heavens the bolt and from the tyrant the scepter." The three allegorical figures at the base of the throne represent (from left to right) Franklin's varied contributions to Literature, Science, and Philosophy.

Medals were struck by Tiffany & Co. in early 1906 in an edition of 151: 1 gold, which was presented to the Republic of France, and 150 bronzes, 100 of which, including this one, were distributed by President Theodore Roosevelt.

KENYON COX (1856–1919)

## 51. Augustus Saint-Gaudens    (fig. 67)
1887 (this replica, 1908)
Oil on canvas, 33½ x 47⅛ in. (85.1 x 119.7 cm)
Gift of friends of the artist, through August F. Jaccaci, 1908 (08.130)

In this, the most significant of the many portraits of Saint-Gaudens, his close friend Kenyon Cox captured the creative and physical vigor of the sculptor. Saint-Gaudens works assuredly at his easel in his Thirty-sixth Street studio, his stance echoing the pose of painter William Merritt Chase in the bas-relief portrait (see fig. 33) he is modeling. He holds a wad of clay and a modeling tool in his left hand. In the shallow background behind him are, at the left, a solar print of Amor, one of the caryatid figures from the Vanderbilt Mantelpiece (cat. 18, fig. 16); at the right, the framed bronze version of his bas-relief portrait of his son Homer (cat. 20, fig. 18); and, at the far right, the scaffolding for the Shaw Memorial (fig. 43). Just to the right of Saint-Gaudens's strong and distinctive profile is a copy of Francesco Laurana's *Femme inconnue* (Musée du Louvre, Paris), a Renaissance sculpture both he and Cox admired. (In his writings on art Cox allied Saint-Gaudens with the great Italian Renaissance masters.)

Cox's original portrait, one of Saint-Gaudens's prized possessions, burned in a fire in 1904 that all but destroyed the contents of the Cornish studio. When the Saint-Gaudens Memorial Committee was

preparing for the exhibition at the Metropolitan in 1908, committee member Cox agreed to make a replica based on a photograph of the original taken by De Witt Ward (the sculptor's preferred photographer for his own works). The cavernous scale of the Great Hall may have led Cox to enlarge the composition to make the figure lifesize. Immediately upon its completion the painting was presented to the Metropolitan through private subscription funds.

ANDERS ZORN (1860–1920)

## 52. Augustus Saint-Gaudens and His Model    (fig. 46)
1897
Etching with retroussage, single state; plate 5⅜ x 7¾ in. (13.7 x 19.8 cm), sheet 9⅞ x 12¾ in. (25.2 x 32.4 cm)
Harris Brisbane Dick Fund, 1917 (17.3.726)

## 53. Augustus Saint-Gaudens
1898
Etching, second state; plate 7¾ x 5⅜ in. (19.7 x 13.5 cm), sheet 13⅞ x 11 in. (35.2 x 27.9 cm)
Harris Brisbane Dick Fund, 1917 (17.3.670)

Swedish-born Anders Zorn was likely introduced to Saint-Gaudens in 1893 during his first visit to the United States, when he came to see the Chicago World's Columbian Exposition. Zorn was one of many artists the sculptor counted amongst the international coterie of friends who provided him both personal and professional comradeship. From time to time the two men shared the same patrons and sitters, among them Frances Folsom Cleveland and Frieda Fanny Schiff (see cats. 31 and 23, and the Metropolitan also owns Zorn's etching of Cleveland and his oil of Schiff).

53

Zorn was celebrated as a painter and watercolorist, but he was also an accomplished etcher, having mastered the technique in the 1880s and completed numerous etched portraits. The first of his etchings of Saint-Gaudens followed a visit to Saint-Gaudens's Twenty-seventh Street studio in New York on February 14, 1897. He depicted the sculptor seated, leaning forward to cede the background to his nude model, who lies propped up on one elbow and gazes outward. She is now identified as Hettie Anderson, the African American model for the figure of Victory in the Sherman Monument (fig. 53). With her reclining pose Zorn (who stored his own etchings in a cabinet alongside his collection of Rembrandt's) was possibly drawing a reference to the figure in Rembrandt's well-known etching *"Negress" Lying Down* of 1658 (Metropolitan Museum).

Zorn produced the second, vertical etching of Saint-Gaudens while he was at the sculptor's Paris studio in December 1898. Again, Saint-Gaudens is shown seated in three-quarter profile, wearing an artist's blouse. Zorn captured the intensity of his features with brisk strokes and a skillful play of projecting lights and receding darks. In the background is a plaster model for *The Puritan* (fig. 26) Saint-Gaudens had shipped from the United States to exhibit in Paris and to use as the basis for reduced versions (see cat. 27). In the etching, reversed from Zorn's original drawing upon the copper plate, the puritan's walking stick appears in his left hand rather than his right.

54, obverse and reverse

JAMES EARLE FRASER (1876–1953)

## 54–55. *Two examples of the Pan-American Exposition Medal to Augustus Saint-Gaudens*
1901
Bronze, diam. of each 3½ in. (9 cm)
Gift of Mr. and Mrs. Frederick S. Wait, 1909 (09.114a, b)

James Earle Fraser was one of Saint-Gaudens's most dedicated and talented studio assistants, working on the Sherman Monument in Paris and, after 1900, in Cornish. After establishing his own studio in New York by 1902, Fraser enjoyed a long and distinguished career as a sculptor of portraits and public monuments. He also achieved considerable success with his numismatic work, including the design for the buffalo nickel, minted between 1913 and 1938.

One of Fraser's earliest medallic efforts was this presentation medal honoring Saint-Gaudens and the sculptures he exhibited in 1901 at the Pan-American Exposition in Buffalo. The obverse presents a naturalistic portrait of Saint-Gaudens in left-facing profile on a herm bust. Both the overall composition and the placement and style of the inscriptions refer not only to Saint-Gaudens's numismatic work but

also to quattrocento examples by Pisanello, whom both Saint-Gaudens and Fraser greatly admired. On the reverse is an allegorical representation of Sculpture standing on mountainous terrain holding a mallet and chisel. Behind him a winged Pegasus—symbolizing the arts—floats aloft. The medal was struck in an edition of twenty-five bronzes. In a letter to Fraser (quoted in the July 1909 issue of the Museum's *Bulletin*, p. 133) Saint-Gaudens called the reverse "one of the finest ideas and arrangements of a medal I have ever seen." Frederick Wait, a major donor of American medals, acquired the Pan-American Exposition Medal directly from Fraser on the Metropolitan's behalf. As was typical, he presented the Museum with two examples so that the obverse and reverse could be viewed at once.

In 1926 Fraser modeled a portrait bust of his former master for the Hall of Fame for Great Americans at New York University (now on the campus of Bronx Community College).

ELLEN EMMET RAND (1875–1941)

## 56. *Augustus Saint-Gaudens*
ca. 1904
Oil on canvas, 38⅞ x 30 in. (98.7 x 76.2 cm)
Rogers Fund, 1908 (08.129)

Ellen Emmet Rand's half-length portrait of a pensive Saint-Gaudens spotlights his distinctive profile and his hands, one dangling his eyeglasses, the other gripping the arm of his chair. His jacket and the background are loosely rendered in a monochromatic palette. The portrait was well received as a faithful likeness not only by Saint-Gaudens and his family but also by his friends, who in 1906 moved to fund its acquisition for the Metropolitan Museum (an effort spearheaded by Charles McKim). Saint-Gaudens's wife and son resisted the proposal on the basis that this was the only extant painted portrait of the sculptor following the devastating Cornish studio fire in 1904, during which Kenyon Cox's 1887 portrait (see cat. 51) and several others had burned.

56

Emmet Rand's portrait was included in Saint-Gaudens's memorial exhibition at the Metropolitan in spring 1908, whereupon in April the Museum purchased it from her in what it believed was good faith. Protracted legal wrangling between Mrs. Saint-Gaudens and the artist ensued, with Mrs. Saint-Gaudens claiming that her husband sat for the portrait on the condition he would assume ownership. In December 1909 she dropped the suit against the Metropolitan (which had become a newsworthy item in the New York press). The Museum gained clear title and retained Saint-Gaudens's portrait, which the Trustees' Executive Committee minutes recorded as "a memorial to him and to his genius." In 1912, with relations normalized, Augusta Saint-Gaudens presented the Metropolitan with the sculptor's relief portrait of Samuel Gray Ward (cat. 17) and subsequently sold the Museum six casts of his work.

Of the three portrait busts of Saint-Gaudens undertaken during his lifetime, Flanagan's best captures both his physical likeness and his emotional intensity. Saint-Gaudens sat for the portrait in Cornish and New York City in 1905. Although by then, as photographs attest, his long struggle with cancer had diminished his robust appearance and spirited demeanor, Flanagan (relying on head measurements and photographs) chose to depict him some years younger, in the vigor of health and at the peak of his creative powers. His is a vital presence, with penetrating eyes, full beard, and prominent nose.

Flanagan's model remained incomplete at the time of Saint-Gaudens's death, and he did not return to the project until 1920, when he received a commission for a portrait of Saint-Gaudens for the Hall of American Artists at New York University. The Metropolitan's bronze was cast in 1924, and a variant one, with clothed shoulders, was completed the following year for New York University (it is now housed at the university's Elmer Holmes Bobst Library).

57

JOHN FLANAGAN (1865–1952)

## 57. Augustus Saint-Gaudens
1905–24 (this cast, 1924)
Bronze, 16½ x 8 x 10 in. (41.9 x 20.3 x 25.4 cm)
Francis Lathrop Fund, 1933 (33.62)

John Flanagan served as a studio assistant to Saint-Gaudens between 1885 and 1890, working on projects that ranged from the *Standing Lincoln* (1884–87; fig. 24) to the George Washington Inaugural Centennial Medal (1889; see cats. 34–35). Like so many aspiring artists of his generation, he then relocated to Paris to continue his studies and take on independent commissions. Flanagan settled in New York in 1902 and earned particular acclaim for his bas-relief portraits and medals.

RUDOLPH RUZICKA (1883–1978)

## 58. Augustus Saint-Gaudens
1907
Color woodcut; block 7⅜ x 6 in. (18.6 x 15.1 cm), sheet 10⅞ x 9 in. (27.6 x 22.7 cm)
Gift of the artist, 1920 (20.80.4)

Czech-born Rudolph Ruzicka emigrated to the United States, probably from Bohemia, in 1894. After apprenticeships in Chicago he moved to New York in 1903 to work as an engraver for the American Bank Note Company, and about 1905 he also studied at the Art Students League. Ruzicka enjoyed a long and prestigious career as a wood engraver, illustrator, and book and typeface designer and is well represented in the Metropolitan's collection.

Among Ruzicka's early efforts is this two-color woodcut portrait of Saint-Gaudens executed in 1907, the year of the sculptor's death. While there is no evidence that the two men were ever acquainted, Ruzicka professed a great admiration for Saint-Gaudens and had certainly seen photographs of him. His profile view is unquestionably adapted from a 1904 studio portrait of Saint-Gaudens taken by De Witt Ward, the sculptor's photographer of choice, in which he sits informally, coat and hat in hand (fig. 71). Ruzicka's rendering of

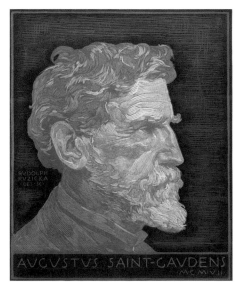

58

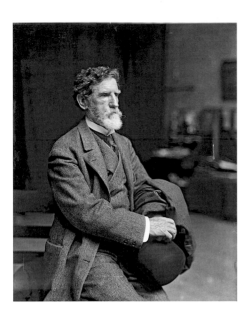

Fig. 71 De Witt Ward. *Saint-Gaudens in His Studio*, 1904. Photograph, mixed media. Smithsonian American Art Museum, Washington, D.C., Peter A. Juley & Son Collection (J0021709)

Saint-Gaudens's wavy hair, bushy eyebrows, and high shirt collar almost exactly matches the photograph, though he oriented the sculptor's head in stricter profile than the three-quarter view of the photograph.

When Ruzicka presented this woodcut to the Metropolitan in 1920 he observed to curator of prints William M. Ivins Jr. that it was the result of youthful experimentation (it was printed in two colors, one laid upon the other to create a third). Ruzicka had contributed the portrait to *A Portfolio of Prints*, issued by the Graphic Arts Club in spring 1908 in an edition of sixty. Technically and compositionally it announces his admiration for Saint-Gaudens's bas-reliefs. The chiaroscuro of the light green striations on the darker background echoes Saint-Gaudens's wispy handling of his relief fields, itself very much indebted to printmaking (see, for instance, cat. 12). Ruzicka's treatment of the inscription, in block letters offset from the rest of the composition, also mimics Saint-Gaudens's trademark style. By signing the woodcut *RVDOLPH RVZICKA ·DES ·SC·* Ruzicka was not only proclaiming himself the designer of the portrait but also allying the reductive process of cutting woodblock prints to the art of sculpture.

## Selected Bibliography

*Augustus Saint-Gaudens, 1848–1907: A Master of American Sculpture*. Exh. cat., Musée des Augustins, Toulouse, and Musée National de la Coopération Franco-Américaine, Château de Blérancourt. Curated by Catherine Gaich and Anne Dopffer. Paris, 1999.

"Augustus Saint-Gaudens: Replicas of His Bas-Reliefs of Children." *Bulletin of The Metropolitan Museum of Art* 1, no. 2 (January 1906), pp. 24–26.

Burdette, Roger W. *Renaissance of American Coinage, 1905–1908*. Great Falls, Va., 2006.

*Catalogue of a Memorial Exhibition of the Works of Augustus Saint-Gaudens*. Exh. cat. New York: The Metropolitan Museum of Art, 1908.

Cortissoz, Royal. *Augustus Saint-Gaudens*. Boston, 1907.

Cox, Kenyon. "Augustus Saint-Gaudens." *Century Illustrated Monthly Magazine* 35 (November 1887), pp. 28–37.

_____. "The Saint-Gaudens Memorial Exhibition." *Bulletin of The Metropolitan Museum of Art* 3, no. 2 (February 1908), pp. 20–21.

Dryfhout, John H. *The Work of Augustus Saint-Gaudens*. Rev. ed. Hanover, N.H., 2008. First published 1982.

Dryfhout, John H., and Beverly Cox. *Augustus Saint-Gaudens: The Portrait Reliefs*. Exh. cat. Washington, D.C.: National Portrait Gallery, Smithsonian Institution, 1969.

Duffy, Henry J., and John Dryfhout. *Augustus Saint-Gaudens: American Sculptor of the Gilded Age*. Exh. cat. Washington, D.C.: Trust for Museum Exhibitions in cooperation with the Saint-Gaudens National Historic Site, Cornish, N.H., 2003.

French, Daniel Chester. "Augustus Saint-Gaudens (1848–1907)." *Proceedings of the American Academy of Arts and Sciences* 53, no. 10 (September 1918), pp. 859–61.

Greenthal, Kathryn. *Augustus Saint-Gaudens: Master Sculptor*. Exh. cat. New York: The Metropolitan Museum of Art, 1985.

Hind, C. Lewis. *Augustus Saint-Gaudens*. New York, 1908.

Marcus, Lois Goldreich. "Studies in Nineteenth-Century American Sculpture: Augustus Saint Gaudens (1848–1907)." Ph.D. diss., City University of New York, 1979.

Moore, Charles. *The Life and Times of Charles McKim*. Boston, 1929.

Moran, Michael. *Striking Change: The Great Artistic Collaboration of Theodore Roosevelt and Augustus Saint-Gaudens*. Atlanta, 2008.

Saint-Gaudens, Augustus. Papers. Rauner Special Collections Library, Dartmouth College, Hanover, N.H.

Saint-Gaudens, Homer, ed. *The Reminiscences of Augustus Saint-Gaudens*. 2 vols. New York, 1913.

"The Saint-Gaudens Exhibition." *Bulletin of The Metropolitan Museum of Art* 3, no. 4 (April 1908), p. 65.

Schiller, Joyce Karen. "The Artistic Collaboration of Augustus Saint-Gaudens and Stanford White." Ph.D. diss., Washington University, Saint Louis, 1997.

Tharp, Louise Hall. *Saint-Gaudens and the Gilded Era*. Boston, 1969.

Tolles, Thayer. "After Saint-Gaudens: His Memorial Exhibition at The Metropolitan Museum of Art." *The Magazine Antiques* 172 (September 2007), pp. 118–29.

_____, as editor. *American Sculpture in The Metropolitan Museum of Art: Volume 1. A Catalogue of Works by Artists Born before 1865*. New York, 1999. For Saint-Gaudens, see pp. 243–325.

_____. "Augustus Saint-Gaudens at The Metropolitan Museum of Art." *Catalogue of Antiques and Fine Art* 4, no. 6 (2004), pp. 248–49.

_____. "Augustus Saint-Gaudens, His Critics, and the New School of American Sculpture, 1875–1893." Ph.D. diss., City University of New York, 2003.

_____. "Daniel Chester French and the Work of Augustus Saint-Gaudens." *The Magazine Antiques* 157 (January 2000), pp. 224–27.

Tomkins, Calvin. *Merchants and Masterpieces: The Story of The Metropolitan Museum of Art*. Rev. ed., New York, 1989. First published 1970.

Tripp, David. *Illegal Tender: Gold, Greed, and the Mystery of the Lost 1933 Double Eagle*. New York, 2004.

White, Samuel G., and Elizabeth White. *Stanford White Architect*. New York, 2008.

Wilkinson, Burke. *Uncommon Clay: The Life and Works of Augustus Saint-Gaudens*. New York, 1985.

## Author's Acknowledgments

Reporting on the opening of Saint-Gaudens's memorial exhibition at the Metropolitan in March 1908, Museum assistant secretary Henry W. Kent wrote to trustee Robert W. de Forest in words that ring aptly true more than one hundred years later with this *Bulletin* and the accompanying exhibition: "It has required the usual scramble to get the work done, and the whole Museum has worked early and late and extra time to accomplish the result." Thayer Tolles acknowledges with gratitude the following individuals at the Metropolitan who offered advice and assistance on this project: Margot Bernstein, Linda Borsch, Einar Brendalen, Bruce Campbell, Aileen Chuk, Meryl Cohen, Martha Deese, Mindell Dubansky, Roberto Ferrari, Barbara File, Morrison H. Heckscher, Jeanie James, Peter Kenny, Daniel Kershaw, Joseph Loh, Catherine Mackay, Constance McPhee, James Moske, John O'Neill, Sue Potter, Catherine Scandalis, Alice Schwarz, Bruce Schwarz, Marjorie Shelley, Linda Sylling, Vanja Vlahovic, Elizabeth Wallace, Barbara Weiss, Christopher Zichello, Egle Zygas, and her American Wing colleagues, notably Karen Lemmey, research associate for this project, and the superb technicians Sean Farrell, Dennis Kaiser, Chad Lemke, and Don Templeton. Additionally, in New Hampshire, Henry Duffy and BJ Dunn at the Saint-Gaudens National Historic Site in Cornish and Jay Satterfield and the staff of the Rauner Special Collections Library at Dartmouth College in Hanover kindly facilitated many rewarding hours of research.